Over the Hill, You Pick Up Speed

Over the Hill, You Pick Up Speed

Reflections on Aging
(For Anyone Who Happens To)

Nardi Reeder Campion

UNIVERSITY PRESS OF NEW ENGLAND

HANOVER AND LONDON

Published by University Press of New England,
One Court Street, Lebanon, NH 03766
www.upne.com
© 2006 by Nardi Reeder Campion
Printed in the United States of America

5 4 3 2 1

Library of Congress Cataloging-in-Publication Data
Campion, Nardi Reeder.
Over the hill, you pick up speed : reflections on aging (for anyone who
happens to) / Nardi Reeder Campion.
  p. cm.
ISBN-13: 978-1-58465-526-8 (cloth : alk. paper)
ISBN-10: 1-58465-526-7 (cloth : alk. paper)
  1. Aging—Humor. I. Title.
PN6231.A43C36 2006
814'.54—dc22   2006000237

The author gratefully acknowledges permission to reprint the following:
From YOU'RE ONLY OLD ONCE! by Dr. Seuss, copyright ™ &
copyright © by Dr. Seuss Enterprises, L.P. 1986. Used by
permission of Random House, Inc.
From *Everyday Miracle*, by Gustav Eckstein, copyright 1948.
Used by permission of HarperCollins Publishers.
Excerpts from "Happiness Makes Up in Height for What It Lacks in Length"
and "New Hampshire" from THE POETRY OF ROBERT FROST edited
by Edward Connery Lathem.
Copyright 1923, 1969 by Henry Holt and Company. Copyright 1951 by
Robert Frost.
Reprinted by permission of Henry Holt and Company, LLC.

FOR MY FAMILY — ORIGINAL, BEGOTTEN, IN-LAW AND
OUT-LAW, EXTENDED AND UNBORN

"Acceptance is magic."

— GUSTAV ECKSTEIN, M.D.

Contents

Contents

The Gratitude Attitude (Condensed)

I'm indebted to so many that this list should be as long as the begats in the Old Testament. I'll limit my thank yous—heartfelt and unwavering—to the biggies: my two brilliant editors, John Landrigan of UPNE and Anne Adams of the *Valley News;* my hard-working and slave-driving writing assistant, Beth Zuttermeister; my mentors, Noel Perrin and Henry Homeyer; my computer freak, Thomas Summerall; and my Tommy, Tad, Toby, Cissa, and Russell, adjunct editors and faithful supporters all.

To the many others who have made this book possible, heartfelt thanks. You know who you are, and so does your helpee.

N.R.C.

Over the Hill, You Pick Up Speed

Introduction

Press On and On

Nothing in the world can take the place of persistence. Talent will not . . . genius will not . . . education will not. Persistence and determination alone are omnipotent. — CALVIN COOLIDGE

Two newspaper pictures are taped to my bathroom wall. One is a stately young black woman in a straw hat, shoulder bag securely in place, shoes in hand, marching through swirling ankle-high water. The caption reads: "Christine Delille crossing the river in Plaine Danger, Haiti. The nurse cares for 2,700 people there and in nearby hamlets." What lifts my spirit is her grace, her matter-of-fact acceptance of her hazardous walk to work, and the cool determination on her face.

The other is a photograph of a young José Clemente Orozco on scaffolding, working on what may be his masterpiece, the frescos in Dartmouth College's Baker Library. The youthful Mexican artist in his knitted cap has a black mustache and that cool look of determination as he stares at his creation, the angry god Quetzalcoatl. This is not simply a photo of genius at work. It epitomizes the triumph of persistence over difficulty. The great muralist Orozco had only one hand. He lost the other in a childhood accident.

I look at Christine and José every day and try to absorb their unquenchable spirit—forge ahead, damn the obstacles.

The obstacle that confronts me daily is aging. Everybody repeats the cliché, "Old age is not for sissies." So what? Naturally there is something wrong with most people my age. I'm deaf, my hands are stiff, my knees don't work, and my memory—well, we won't go into that. Who knows what will go next? These two photographs show me that one can every day confront overwhelming obstacles with acceptance and determination.

As everybody knows, there are strategies that ease aging. Taking care of your health, for example. I strive to adhere to the usual health rules: walk every day, drink lots of water, skip fried food, eat fresh fruit and raw vegetables, nap every afternoon (that's easy), enjoy reading, music, and other people (not always easy). Years ago my husband and I quit smoking and drinking. Luckily. But what really keeps me going is writing.

The secret to accepting aging, I think, is a project you are passionate about. I have a friend who knits for charity and listens to book tapes at the same time. She can hardly wait to get back to it. Another friend does telephoning for her church and enjoys keeping in touch. My dear friend Bonnie Westcott played the piano for people to sing along at the weekly social hour at Harvest Hill, my retirement community in Lebanon, New Hampshire. Obstacles were nothing to Bonnie. She is blind. She told me, "The new resident just asked me, 'Are you going to the social hour? I hear they've got an old blind lady who plays the piano.'" We both thought that was funny.

Laughter may be the best strategy of all.

My mother's mantra was: "Example is not the best way to teach. It is the only way to teach." My husband, Tom, taught me by example to laugh at the indignities of old age. As he said, they *are* funny, if you stop to think about it. How did we get this way so fast? Tom, who had thyroid problems, balance problems, and heart problems, went steadily downhill for two years until he died in November 2000. But he never lost the gift of laughter.

He didn't just laugh at aging. He lived his life with laughter.

We raised our five children through trial and error and humor. The kids turned out all right (an understatement).

I have tried to follow Tom's spirited example. After we moved to Hanover, New Hampshire, a wonderful thing happened. Tom's old friend Bin Lewis, editor of the *Valley News* of West Lebanon, New Hampshire, invited me to write a column for his paper. On April 4, 1987, "Everyday Matters" was born. If you want to learn to write short—an invaluable skill—a newspaper column is the place to begin.

As I said, what keeps me going is writing. I always planned to write the story of my life. I kept diaries and voluminous notebooks, thinking, "If I get the time, I'll have the material." When I finally sat down to read them I got a terrible shock. Only one word describes those diaries: boring. As Oscar Wilde said, "Telling every detail is the definition of boring." I placed the journals back on the shelf, and there they vegetate.

My English Comp professor at Wellesley College, Miss Elizabeth Manwaring, required us to read Helen Keller's *The Story of My Life*. Here was a woman who became deaf and blind at nineteen months old. Her autobiography is short, simple, and powerful. The astonishing Miss Keller wrote, "We can do anything we want to do if we stick to it long enough."

As the years rolled along I struggled over my own autobiography. Every New Year's Eve in our family we asked the same question and wrote down the answer: "What do you want to do in the coming year?" Not a New Year's resolution but a reality check. What exactly do you plan to *do?* I always said the same thing: "Finish my book." ("ME-more," my husband called it.)

It was slow going. Tom edited my first chapters and said, tactfully, "Persistence pays off. Soldier on, Joan of Arc." I bolstered myself by sitting at my typewriter (*sic*) and repeating my brother Colonel Red Reeder's motto—and, later, epitaph— "Never quit: press on and on." I pressed on and on, to no avail.

Tom said, "At your age, you need a writing assistant." As usual, he was right. Leyla Kamalick, a Dartmouth student, guided me into the computer age. She and I worked together on my ME-more for four years, and then she selfishly graduated and went off to teach English at Andover.

And Tom left me, too.

Lost, I stopped trying to write. But the urge never died. At long last I began to look for another helper. I asked one applicant, a high school senior, "Can you take dictation?" She said, "What's that?"

Thanks to my therapist, Mollie Brooks, Beth Zuttermeister, mother of four-year-old twins, took me over. When you're past eighty, a good assistant makes all the difference. Beth unscrambles my files, finds my lost papers, takes dictation, manages my computer, and bosses me around. I need a lot of bossing.

There's such a thing as being "over-determined." But not with Beth. She'll say, "All right, that's enough for today. Go take your rest." Then one day Beth shook me up. She announced, "Don't look now, but I think you've finished your memoir." I could not believe it, but as usual Beth was right.

Then came the burning question: how to get published? I had published seven books, but nobody who knew me was left at Little Brown or Holt Rinehart. "Try University Press of New England," my prolific garden writer friend, Henry Homeyer, suggested.

Beth and I put together a submission packet for UPNE. Granddaughter Ashley said, "You already have a title: *Everyday Matters.*" Friend Sara Coburn suggested the subtitle: "*A Love Story.*"

I took the manuscript to UPNE, conveniently located here in Lebanon. Richard Abel, UPNE's director, invited me to confer with him and editor John Landrigan. "This isn't at all what I expected," Richard said. "I thought your book was a collection of columns. Have you finished the whole thing?"

"Yes—and it about finished me."

"How soon can we see it?"

"This afternoon?"

To cut a blissful story short, they offered me a modest contract. (I did not mention that I would have paid them to publish it.) I hesitated, briefly. "It has to be hardback. This is my legacy to our kids—and their kids." They nodded and I felt my heartbeat increase. "I'm one-hundred-ten years old. How soon can you publish it?"

"Under the circumstances," John said, "I think we should get it out by next October, in time for the Christmas market."

I grinned. "Great, but it would probably sell better posthumously." John chuckled.

I waltzed home, delirious with joy. If *only* Tom were here to waltz with me. I'd been working on the damned book forever. Helen Keller had it right. "We can do anything we want to do if we stick to it long enough."

Everyday Matters: A Love Story was published in October 2004, when I was eighty-seven. (Oh, to be eighty-seven again.)

Yes, President Coolidge. Nothing can take the place of persistence. It pays off. And nothing is more persistent than aging. It's unstoppable. The calm acceptance of Christine Delille wading to work in Plaine Danger, Haiti, and the determination of Orozco in creating a masterpiece with one hand prove that obstacles can make us stronger. Determination and acceptance are crucial.

I don't know what I think about anything until I write it down. That's how this book came about. I needed answers to three questions. Who was that strange-looking character in the mirror? How did she get that way? How does she really feel about growing old? Answer: Read on.

Misadventures in Aging

Dear Reader, as the Brontës used to say, let me introduce myself. I am an eighty-eight-year-old (at last count) mother, grandmother, great-grandmother, Republican-turned-Democrat, cradle Episcopalian, army brat, born Reeder (in the true sense of the word), Wellesley alum, author of nine books, arthritic sportswoman, lover of good conversation, and bereft widow.

My first—and only—husband and I married in 1941 and survived five children (Tom, a lawyer in Idaho; Tad, an M.D. in Boston; Toby, a chiropractor/writer in L.A.; Cissa, a musician/composer in Boston; and Russell, an investor in Chicago), the arrival of eight grandchildren, the divorces of three children, the apotheosis of two great-grandchildren, umpteen pets and crises, and five moves. If you make it to the end of the book, you'll know more than you need to know about my family.

In 1978, my husband accepted the challenge of creating the Parents Fund at Dartmouth College. We moved to the Upper Valley, comprised of several towns along the Connecticut River in both Vermont and New Hampshire.

We lived in Hanover, New Hampshire, until August 2000, when we moved to Harvest Hill Retirement Community. Tom died in November 2000. The Upper Valley is a good place to grow old—if you like cold weather. I love it.

For me, getting older is less threatening when I write and, hopefully, laugh about it. Aging is like going over Niagara in a barrel: there's no way to stop it. You might as well profit from the trip. In life there is nothing else like it.

Why I Stopped Driving My Car

The response to this "Everyday Matters" column surprised me. Many young people called to ask, "How can I get a copy of your column about giving up your car? I need to send it to my parents."

In America, people think of driving as a God-given right. The cold fact that old people hate to face is: we all have to stop driving someday. Figuring out when "someday" comes is the hard part.

Don't do as I did—wait until it's almost too late.

My doctor son presented me with free taxi coupons. I got the message but I was not ready to stop driving. "Mom," he said, "you *are* getting older."

"Yes, and in eighty-six years I've never had an accident. I'll know when it's time to stop. Your father thought I was an excellent driver."

No answer.

I did sign up for the "AARP 55 Alive Safe Driving Course." You don't have to belong to AARP and it costs only ten dollars. Two mornings, eight hours total, led by David Minsk of Hanover, a good teacher. He knew the program was important.

"Why are you here?" he asked the blonde who looked about thirteen. "The policeman sent me because I kept my eyes on the road instead of the speedometer." A truck driver in a black tee-shirt with American flags muttered, "Same here, lady."

I learned a lot in safe driving school. (Q: Where do most older people have accidents? A: At intersections.) One thing the teacher said rocked me: "You are going to have to stop driving someday. Better to make the choice yourself than to have someone else make it for you."

It had never occurred to me that I would have to stop driving. But I still didn't take it in. That applies to older people, I thought. After "graduation" I bought a high pillow to sit on and increase my vision, gave up driving at night, and enjoyed my new confidence.

Then I had a nightmare of an accident. Here's how it happened:

I was going to the hospital for my doctor to check me out to see if I should accept my nephew's invitation to take a trip to Paris and Normandy. Instead of seeing Dr. Ross, I ended up in the emergency room.

As I was approaching the entrance of the hospital, I slowed down near valet parking. Suddenly—without warning—my car shot forward, fast. The gas pedal was stuck. I plowed into a parked car ahead of me, but kept going. Ahead, I saw people frozen in their tracks. Thinking my brakes had failed, I swerved and drove into a hospital pillar to stop. I turned off the engine and sat holding my head in my hands. I couldn't believe what had happened.

I could hear the man whose car I hit saying in a Vermont voice, "I was sittin' quietly, waitin' for my wife, and BANG— there goes my rear end."

He laughed. How could anybody laugh at a time like this? I stared at him. Not much younger than I, he had curly white hair and a mustache, and even at a distance I could see his eyes twinkling.

Hospitals are expert at emergencies. The attendants swung into action and minutes later my cheery victim and I were wheeled into the emergency room. The physician's assistant gave each of us a going over and applauded us for wearing seatbelts. The Vermonter had a sore shoulder, that was all. Even our blood pressures were okay. At that point the wife he'd been waiting for was wheeled in and he started telling her what happened. I took out my hearing aids; I couldn't bear to listen. His wife smiled and waved at me. Amazing. Had I been in her place, I would have bopped me.

Dr. Ross came out to meet me when I arrived by wheelchair (once you get in one, they never let you out). I felt a bit woozy but I wasn't shaking. "My brakes failed," I began. He said, "They called me. It's lucky the hospital is still standing." Dr. Ross pronounced me unharmed. As I was leaving he said, "There's a policeman waiting to see you." Uh-oh.

Patrol Officer Dustin Adams of the Lebanon Police Department was a clean-cut young man with a gentle manner. I told him what I thought had happened and he said, "Your car left black skid marks on the concrete."

"How could that be? I was going slowly when the foot pedal stuck . . . "

Officer Adams said gently, "Do you think you might have stepped on the gas instead of the brake?"

I just stared at him.

My friend Jim Leech, who has driven me before, took me home to Harvest Hill. That afternoon I talked to insurance people, AAA (bless their hearts), body shops, and so on, but I could not bring myself to tell my family what I had done. Utterly depressed, I did something I never do. I took a sleeping pill and went to bed at seven.

I woke up early and did a lot of pondering. No one was hurt, thank the Lord. Think about that poor old fellow (about my age) who stepped on the gas instead of the brake in a California farmer's market and killed eleven people.

Suddenly it all came clear. I had driven a car for the last time.

The greatest day in the life of a teenager is the day she gets her license. The worst day in the life of an oldager is the day she gives up her license. Driving equals independence. But the funny thing is, after I decided it was time to quit driving forever, my feeling of gloom and doom lifted. So what if I lose my independence? Some things are more important, such as not killing anybody. Suddenly I felt lighthearted. Already I was saving lives.

Acceptance is magic.

My phone rang and a voice said, "This is Clara Burnham in White Rivah. My husband, Roger, was sittin' in our car when you bumped it. We just called to find out how you're feelin' and tell you don't fret. It could happen to anyone." I could have hugged both of them.

Maybe it wasn't an accident. Maybe it was a Teachable Moment. It taught me to say to my son the doctor—with feeling—the hardest sentence in the English language: "I was wrong." (Tad eschewed the dreaded "I told you so"—or said it too low for me to hear.)

In all the excitement I had forgotten to ask Dr. Ross about going to France in the spring. I telephoned. "Do you think I'm up to the Paris and Normandy trip?"

"Well," he said, "you passed the stress test."

Twelve Ways to Get Around Without a Car

Guess who said "Imagination is more important than knowl-edge." Walt Disney? J. K. Rowling? No. It was someone renowned for knowledge: Albert Einstein.

Einstein's wisdom surfaced in a book review, just when I needed it. After my accident, I sold the offending car. Now what? I had no idea how to proceed without a car.

"Okay, Dr. E," I said. "I'll give it a try." Carless in Lebanon, I closed my eyes and summoned my imagination. Was it up to the job? Doubtful. As always, I made a list. (I could hear Tom saying, "You ought to keep a list of your lists.")

Saying good-bye to my Honda was a jolt. Everybody kept asking, "How do you get around without a car?" As if I knew.

I consulted my new situation and made another list. Pluses: no car insurance, no licenses to renew, no oil to change, no tires to check, no garage rental, no parking problems, and I don't care how much gas goes up (always thinking of others). Of course there was one minus and it was huge: independence gonzo.

Trying to get where I want to go, I've explored various options. Some are good; some, as the Godfather says, "Notsa guda." One is glorious. Here is my Possibility List.

1. Public Transportation: Miraculously, the Upper Valley offers free bus service. It provides 275,000 rides per year, one

of the best ideas ever. Riding Advance Transit is like joining a club—everybody is your friend. I pick it up in Lebanon and get off at the Hanover Inn or sometimes at the hospital. The brisk walks to and from the stops are good for me, even if I do have to sit down and rest on steps along the way.

2. Taxi: Surprisingly easy, reliable, and reasonable (by Boston standards). But you have to plan ahead, not my strong suit. Never expect to get a cab on the spur of the moment (formerly my strong suit.)

3. Helpful Friends: They all called to offer help. And they do, cheerfully. But one wants to hang on to friends, not exhaust them. Most invitations now include "someone will pick you up," and that's nice.

4. Harvest Hill Van and Drivers: Most retirement homes offer a free van at regular times for residents. Harvest Hill also has Jim and Joe, two charming young men who do everything, including chauffeuring for a nominal fee.

5. Bicycle: Not recommended; I fell off mine. FOR SALE: Vintage 1969 "girl's" Raleigh with three baskets. A collector's item.

6. Roller Skates: Out. Not since I turned seventy.

7. Motor Scooter: Tempting, but too dangerous.

8. Shanks' Mare: I always wondered about that expression. We—that is Beth, my writing assistant—Googled it. Online Word Detective reports, with a touch of humor: "'Shanks' mare' means relying on your own legs for locomotion, better known as walking; 'shanks' pony.' More common in Britain, has been around since 1774. Even older is 'taking walker's bus.' Of course, the humor found in sayings like these may be dependent on whether you are the one faced with the long walk." Ha, ha, ha, ha.

9. Horseback: I grew up in the Old Army, B.T. (before tanks); we rode horses every day. I yearned to live like Robert

Moses. When he was Transportation Czar of New York, his employees cut a bridle path through the Long Island woods from his home to his office, so the Great Man could ride to work. Lacking my own bridle path—and a horse—I must eschew horseback.

10. Don't Go: Just mutter "Been there, done that," stay home, and relax. Read those delicious-looking books that have piled up, waiting—unless, like me, you hate to miss anything.

11. Hitchhiking: My kids said, "Don't you dare, Mom." But why not? When I was in college, everybody hitchhiked. We were heavily influenced by Clark Gable and Claudette Colbert in *It Happened One Night*.

The first time Tom came to Virginia to meet my family, he hitchhiked from Ohio. My parents would have been horrified, had they known. I made him promise to board the Chesapeake & Ohio in Hampton. Ten minutes later he got off in Phoebus, where my mother and I met him. "I'm glad to be here," Tom said with a wide grin. "It was a long trip."

Since I achieved car-lessness, I've hitchhiked three times. The first time it was raining. A nice young man instantly picked me up and took me halfway. He turned out to be a Dartmouth classmate of our youngest son, Russell, but he was late and couldn't take me far. Seeing me hitching in the rain, the next car stopped. A kind woman went out of her way to take me to Veronique, my massage therapist. I said to myself, "Hitching is the way to go. There's nothing to it."

The third time cured me. Wouldn't you think people would stop for an old lady smiling and waving her thumb, her white hair shining in the sun? Forget it. Car after car zipped by without even slowing down. The rain must be essential.

Discouraged, I whipped out my cell phone. Battery dead. (So what else is new?) I waved my thumb for twenty minutes as cars zipped by. I was giving out when I saw a young woman climb into a parked car. I ran over and stuck my head in the window. "I'll give you ten dollars to take me to Lebanon." She laughed. "I'll take you for nothing." Tatum Simon turned out to be a Harvard graduate and resident in radiology who was getting married in four days to an engineer at a big wedding in New Orleans. They both had after-graduation jobs waiting in St. Louis.

When we reached Harvest Hill, I said, "I know you won't take money, Tatum, but I have something for you." I autographed a copy of *Everyday Matters: A Love Story* to her. She was amazed. So was I.

12. Private Chauffeur: Our five kids, who call me the Unguided Missile, were so pleased I finally quit driving that they got together and established "Mom's Taxi Fund," a generous account only to use for being driven. "We don't want you ever to have to say you can't go somewhere because you can't get there," they told me. I was, to put it mildly, overwhelmed.

Luckily, I knew Jim Leech, who had just retired as director of Dartmouth College Printing. Living nearby, Jim agreed to be ever-ready for a reasonable sum per hour. He calls it "Driving Miss Nardi." If we're going as far as Boston, I doze in the back seat with his pillow and blanket while listening to Mozart. This solution is glorious, even sublime.

All in all, I hardly miss Herr Honda. I get where I need to go, I'm meeting nice people, and I am certainly safer. Some say the Upper Valley is safer, too.

How to Improve Your Memory, Maybe

All my life I've fallen for "How To" courses, the weakness of a born optimist. My worst failure was "How to Take Shorthand." No matter how I tried, those little squiggles meant nothing. My best success was "How to Type," which I took at night school when our kids were little. Why did I ever pay my roommate Mouse Matthews five cents per page to type all my papers in college? I won't even discuss "How to Master Your Macintosh," a Dartmouth course for beginners; thirteen years later, I'm still a beginner.

When we retirees at Harvest Hill were offered an eight-week course called "How to Improve Your Memory," I signed up, naturally. Most of the class was over eighty, some of us way over.

For me, memory is the thing I forget with. I forget everything. Dinner dates, birthdays, keys, names (especially names), diets, doctor's appointments, where I put my glasses (that's the worst), and everything else.

Our teacher, Bruce Shinn of Lebanon College, remembers everything, especially quotes, ranging from Will Rogers ("Never slap a man who's chewing tobacco") to Einstein ("Imagination is more important than knowledge").

"The study of ancient cultures that had no written language," he instructed us, "proves that storytelling is the best memory aid. Motivation comes next. You have to *want* to remember." That's why I can't remember where I put the keys. I don't want the damn things. I hate keys.

He teaches mnemonics, using the old chestnuts: "Roy G. Biv" to recall the colors of the rainbow, and "HOMES" for the Great Lakes, a lame mnemonic because the lakes are not in order. On a map, Superior comes first, Ontario last. "Order," our teacher stressed, "is everything."

I protested. "I can't do order."

"Of course you can," he said, "if you keep going over the list. You must repeat an ordered list out loud at least five times in the same sequence to move it into your long-term memory." Five is not enough for me. The Catholic Church stresses nine, as in the Novena, a prayer that is repeated nine times each day for nine days. After that it's yours for keeps.

Our teacher must have been discouraged by the way our second session began. Lois jumped up, exclaiming, "I'll be back, I forgot my hearing aid." Whereupon I jumped up. "I forgot my hearing aid, too." Later I said, "So much for motivation. Both of us wanted to hear your class." Teacher laughed, "Maybe you don't love your hearing aids."

I've already used one of Teacher's tips to advantage. "You must have a peg to hang what you want to remember on. A peg is something you know well and the more ridiculous the connection between the peg and your memory picture, the better. Add action and you'll have it. In kinesthetic learning, you say it OUT LOUD as you act it."

I can't ever remember which knobs control the rear burners on my stove because my old stove was different, so I held a Rear Burner Drill. I stood in front of the stove, placing each hand on a rear knob. Then with both hands I slapped something I know well: my rear end. I kept doing that—knobs, rear-end slap; knobs, rear-end slap—until it became automatic. This may be worth the whole course, because we all know what can happen when you turn on the wrong burner. I'll never make that mistake again. I hope.

"Verbalization, imagination, and visualization are crucial," our teacher said. "If you can combine them with action, they are invaluable. In memorizing, make a picture in your mind using all four. The more absurd the picture is, the easier it will be to recall."

ENEMIES OF MEMORY
1. Fatigue
2. Stress
3. Speed
4. Alcohol
5. Routine (If you've always left your keys on the hall table, and move them elsewhere, you will create a problem.)

FRIENDS OF MEMORY
1. Motivation
2. Attention
3. Association
4. Imagination (the wilder your association, the better)
5. Repetition—OUT LOUD
6. Routine (If you always do something the same way, it eventually becomes automatic. This can be useful.)

Our homework was to learn a poem. "To memorize," Teacher said, "you must be well-rested. Strive for placidness, draining away stress. Stress blocks memory."

I chose Emily Dickinson's *Papa Above, Regard a Mouse;* it's short and visual and I love Emily. It was easy to picture a huge white cat pouncing on a little gray mouse. Then the mouse escaping to nibble all day in a snug cupboard, while God attended to the Cycles, wheeling away.

I repeated Emily's poem over and over out loud, in a rhythmic sing-song voice (verbalization). Now I can (and do) recite it at the drop of a hat.

"Never forget that with memory, motivation is everything," repeated Teacher. "If you *want* to remember something badly enough, you will. And when you do recall it, enjoy your success. That's important."

Ever the showoff, I held up my hand. "Dr. Johnson said, 'No man ever forgot the name of his dog or his mistress.'"

Cliff Procter, wit, lawyer, crossword puzzler, spoke up from the back of the room. "Well," he observed, speaking slowly, "that all depends on how many of each you have."

The Game of the Name

The gingko tree is known as the tree of memory. Darwin called it "the living fossil." That's me. I'm a living fossil and a ginkgo addict as well. Thanks to my son the chiropractor, I take three strong ginkgo pills every day, and I'm convinced that it helps my memory. My son the doctor says, "Keep thinking that. The placebo effect is powerful."

Most older people mistrust their memory. Some of us worry more than others, but we all wonder about our reliability, especially with names. I was happy to discover that even at my age, something can be done about the name problem.

I used to think I had a disease because I can't remember names. Once you forget a friend's name, the friend never forgets you forgot it. Some pretend it doesn't matter, some kid you, some sulk—all remember. And you do, too, especially in the middle of the night.

I lack Huckleberry Finn's ingenuity. Awakening at the Graingerford's, he could not remember the phony name he had made up for himself the night before. Always nimble-witted, Huck teased Buck Graingerford, "I bet you can't spell my name." Buck said, "G-o-r-g-e J-a-x-o-n," and Huck "set it down private" so he could rattle it off like he was used to it.

I once tried the Huck Finn ploy and bombed out. "How do you spell your name?" I asked. The acid answer: "The same way everybody else spells Black."

Recently I saw a good friend coming toward me at the grocery store and I froze. Her name had vanished from my screen.

Sickening. I escaped down another aisle. By the time her name resurfaced, she was gone.

I took my name crisis to our memory teacher. "Memory is like knitting," Bruce Shinn said. "If you don't work on it, it won't grow." He gave us tips on the art of remembering names. Now all I have to do is remember the tips.

"To remember names, verbalize, locate, repeat, associate, and then peg. Repeat several times in the next few minutes. The short-term memory is tricky. We lose fifty percent of what we learn in the first twenty-four hours. You must keep going over and over it to move it into long-term memory."

A perfect example of the importance of repetition is something everybody has done: learning to tie shoelaces. Hard at first, easier with each repetition, eventually automatic.

Teacher said, "I want to stress that stress is a memory blocker." That made me think about my friend Betty. She had just married Lester Smith when her father invited his only child's new husband to meet his friends at the club. Afterward, the groom told the bride, "Please tell your father my name is Smith, not Jones."

Stress certainly undid my niece Dodie Hruby when she was a brand-new bride. A clerk asked for her name and she burst into tears. She had to rush into the ladies room to check her driver's license.

If you take time to relax, I learned, the name will usually come. Teacher gave us a prescription for recalling a name.

1. Go to bed visualizing the person.
2. When you first wake up, rested and relaxed, presto! The name floats out of the Nowhere into the Here. We hope.

In the name game, as in most games, the winner is the one with a sharp, pure focus. "The key to remembering a new name," Teacher said, "is listening, and listening is the art of attention."

That's my problem. Sometimes when I'm introduced I don't even hear the name because my attention is elsewhere. My friend Janet Dakin Wilder, sister of Thornton Wilder and brilliant teacher at Mount Holyoke, once told me blithely, "I never remember names. Not a priority."

"With memory, as with all achievement," Teacher said, repeating his favorite dictum, "motivation is everything. You have to hear the name correctly, then motivate yourself to move it into your memory."

AVV is my mnemonic for name recall:

1. Assign the face to a location you already know.
2. Verbalize (repeat).
3. Visualize (make an exaggerated image).

I met a man named Frank. "How are you, Frank?" I asked. "Where are you from, Frank? (Locate.) New Jersey? Was Jersey always your home, Frank?" (Repeat.) Later I said to myself, "I'll never forget Frank. He has dark hair, dark eyes, and a wide smile. Grew up in Montclair and his name is . . . er . . . ah . . . oh damn it all, what *is* his name?" (Had I pegged him on my beloved nephew Frank, I'd know it. Maybe.)

I told the teacher his system didn't work for me. "Maybe you lack motivation," he said. "No way," I said. "I wanted to remember his name." Then I had to laugh. "But not very much."

Shakespeare, Dickens, Shaw, and others get laughs every time a pompous character is addressed by a screwy version of his name. In real life, a rose by any other name does not smell as sweet; it just smells.

Groucho Marx, the "Insultist," told one of his TV guests, "I never forget a face, but in your case I'll be glad to make an exception." To remember a face: look at the person intently and take a mental photograph. Then imagine a ridiculous exaggeration of one feature. Say to yourself, "Joe's heavy eyebrows are so thick he can't see out." Repeat several times, seeing Joe in your mind's eye until you're sure you have it for good.

In the name game, honesty may be the worst policy. I found that out the hard way. When a woman in our church complained that I never knew her, I was forthright. "Tell me your name," I answered. "I promise I'll remember it." She snapped, "That's what you said the last time." To people who use the terrible ploy "I bet you don't know who I am," I simply lie, "I never bet."

Probably only Winston Churchill, who knew everything and everybody, could get away with the truth. Greeted warmly by an unfamiliar face, he replied, "Sir, one of the few advantages of age is that you can be more open about your defects. Who the hell are you?"

Dartmouth Professor Noel Perrin, my dear friend and mentor, once told me about a relative of his, who as befits our topic shall remain nameless. Nameless proved that absolutely the worst solution is bluffing. The man panicked when a woman sat beside him on a commuter train because he could not dredge up her name. She mentioned her brother and, clutching at straws, he asked, "What is your dear brother doing these days?" She gave him a look. "Oh, he's still president of the United States."

I'm a Loser

I myself find it hard to believe I have lost so much stuff. Over the years I have lost keys, birth certificates, silverware, gloves (hundreds), lists (daily), checks, cash, glasses, engagement calendars (that's the worst). I lost a car title and registration, one dog, two cats, a leg of lamb (cooked), ration books (World War II), critical phone numbers, a fur hat, an automobile (towed), and, naturally, my temper. I even lost a child once, but he was returned by the floor walker.

When I discussed my problem with my therapist, she asked, "Do you try to do things too fast? Are you easily distracted? Do you check and doublecheck everything? Or are you apt to be a little slapdash?" The answers: Yes, yes, no, yes. But there is a fringe benefit to being a loser. Read on.

❦

One summer my red wallet vanished while Tom and I were dining at an inn in Chelsea, Vermont. I knew the wallet had been stolen; I just didn't know where or how. Endless searching, aided by the innkeeper, turned up no clues.

The next day Tom said, "You have to cancel all those credit cards and get a new license." Moaning and groaning, I spent days on that rotten ritual.

No way to replace the money, of course. I don't normally carry one hundred forty dollars, but on that day I had just been to the bank. Oh, misery.

Some time later I received a strange phone call. "This is Mary Merchand in White River Junction. Did you by any chance donate a black leather pocketbook to the St. Thomas rummage sale?"

I said that I had.

She went on: "Last night I was showing my husband my rummage sale bargains. I held up your purse and said, 'Look at all these compartments.' I started unzipping them—and discovered some money. I found a card with your name and looked you up in the phone book. I've called several times. I want to return your money."

I was stunned. "It's yours now," I said slowly. "Losers weepers, finders keepers."

"Oh, no. The cash belongs to you. I wouldn't feel right about keeping it. Can you come to Dartmouth Christian Fellowship School in West Lebanon where I teach, so I can return it?"

My mind went back to a "telefraud" article: *Beware of the Unknown Caller who says he/she has found something of yours.* Should I trust her? Aloud I said, "You must be that one person in a thousand who is totally honest."

She sounded surprised. "Why, anybody would return it."

When I told Tom he said, "She sounds too good to be true."

I met Mary Merchand at her school, a slender woman with lots of dark hair who looks younger than her students. To meet her is to trust her. With a shy smile, she handed me her rummage sale bonanza. "My husband wants to know how you define rummage." We both laughed.

When I saw Mary's find, I almost fell over. There was the red wallet I was sure had been stolen months earlier. Inside were my credit cards, my driver's license, and one hundred forty dollars. I must have unconsciously zipped the wallet into a hidden pocket in my purse. Unconscious is the right word. If

you were searching for a word to describe yours truly, unconscious would spring to the lips.

I opened the infamous red wallet and made a contribution
to the Dartmouth Christian Fellowship School in Mary Merchand's honor. People like Mary make losing worthwhile.

Well, almost.

Losing gets worse with aging, of course. Something new
and terrible has been added to my I'm-a-Loser List: my all-
important, highly expensive hearing aid.

I put off getting a hearing aid as long as I could. "You don't
mind wearing glasses," Tom said gently. "Why worry about a
hearing aid?"

"Young people wear glasses. Old people wear hearing aids."

"Well?" He laughed.

Doctor Tad advised, "You'll be thankful you did it, Mom.
But remember, there is no such thing as a cheap hearing aid.
Get the best." My ever-indulgent husband said, "Tad's right."
He patted my hand. "You buy, I'll pay."

Mother knows best, right? Wrong. I bought the less expensive hearing aid. Emily Dickinson wrote, "Everybody says
'what?' to me." With that first hearing aid, I said 'what?' to
everybody. One inexpensive and one medium-priced hearing
aid later, I finally invested in the best.

Invested is the right word. The hearing aid, which was ad-
vertised as "the smallest digital hearing instrument the world
has ever seen" had the biggest price the world has ever seen.
Tom said, "Forget the cost." He paid the bill and then he died.
No connection (I think).

A year slipped by. On Thanksgiving I got down on my knees
and gave thanks for Tom. All ears, as they say, I set off to spend
the holiday with our children in Boston. There were only five
other people on the Dartmouth Coach headed for Logan Airport. I was able to stretch out on the long back seat and snooze.

Usually a star napper, I could not cork off. What was that loud noise? I finally realized my stellar hearing aid was over-amplifying the roar of traffic. I took the tiny hearing aids out, put them carefully into the little pouch made for that purpose, and slept my way to Boston. A quick trip.

That evening at my son's house, I opened the pouch to pull out the magic ear-mikes. Ye gods! Only the red right one was there. Where was the blue left one? Missing, that's where. How *could* I have lost it? It had to be on the bus. Oh, horrible, horrible, and yet again horrible. My hearing aid was so small and the bus was so big. I felt sick to my stomach.

Frantically, I telephoned the Lebanon office of the Dartmouth Coach. The woman who answered was sympathetic. "That bus should be back here in about ten minutes. We'll search for your hearing aid."

I was a wreck. I could not bring myself to tell my kids about it. I didn't want them to know their mother was a bubble-head. Laughing and nodding through our feast, I pretended I knew what they were talking about. We were eating warm pumpkin pie and sipping hot coffee when the phone rang. Tad excused himself. He returned quickly. "Did you lose your hearing aid?"

I looked up and said, "What?"

"DID YOU LOSE YOUR NEW HEARING AID?"

I lowered my eyes. "I'm afraid I did."

"Well, this man says he found it. It was between the back cushions of the bus. However did it get there?" I still don't know.

There are few joys in life that can equal finding a lost treasure. And if it is something you can't afford to replace, the Joy of Finding goes over the top.

Everybody's Worst Travel Nightmare

I once sat next to E. B. White at a party—and I'm still talking about it. "People will pay good money for clearly written accounts of other people's disasters," he told me.

Travel over eighty can be fraught. Disaster doesn't even begin to describe my Thanksgiving visit to California.

Everybody's worst nightmare is sitting in an airport and watching your plane depart without you. It shouldn't happen to a dog, but it happened to me during a Thanksgiving holiday in California.

My misadventures began the day before Thanksgiving. Ned Perrin used to tell me when I took a trip, "Try to have an adventure." Easy for an Unguided Missile.

I recalled Ned's advice as I lay in the emergency room of Alhambra Hospital in Los Angeles, squeezing son Toby's hand. It was the day before Thanksgiving. Maybe I didn't fully appreciate Toby until that moment. His healing power is awesome, in the true sense of that overworked word.

Toby, the rebellious middle child, was not pure bliss to raise. If that's what we did; in a sense, he raised us. Toby in a capsule: president and captain of everything in high school; sailed off to Harvard (Class of 1970); dropped out junior year to protest the Vietnam War; worked for VISTA in a St. Louis ghetto; lived with his Mexican yoga teacher, Anita; married her, giving us a beloved daughter-in-law and grandchildren Manolo and Iris; opened a new age bookstore in the Ozarks (not a winning proposition); attended the National College of Chiropractic in Chicago for four years; moved his family to Cuzco, Peru, for two years while he and Anita worked as missionaries for the Universal Great Brotherhood. Today Toby is a highly regarded chiropractor/poet/yoga teacher/screenwriter in L.A.

How did I end up in the E.R.? It wasn't easy.

On my way to mail a letter, I stubbed my toe on a broken sidewalk and fell forward. Everything went into slow motion. Crash! My forehead hit the cement and my head bounced.

A stranger named Cathy Wills Abbey saw me fall, hit the brakes, jumped out, and called 911 on her cell. I lay on the sidewalk without moving, taking stock. Still conscious, teeth intact, eyes focused, able to move but afraid to. Slowly, I rolled over, my bleeding face dripping. So far, so good. Good Samaritan was amazed I could remember my son's phone number. (It's the only number I can remember—1776).

The emergency squad roared up. "What is your name? Date of birth?" I was fine with that. "Who is president?" I hesitated. "Do I have to say?" Toby and Anita arrived. I was lying flat, still bleeding. Toby, awed, said, "You're tough, Mom." "I have to be," I whispered.

They had been at home packing because we were leaving in two hours to spend Thanksgiving with our dear friends, Melissa Keeler and Mike Morris, at their ranch high above Santa Barbara. We had to leave L.A. before traffic rigor mortis set in.

I said to Toby, "Nowadays people go to emergency rooms and stay three days. I've wrecked everybody's Thanksgiving."

He patted my hand: "The only thing that matters, Mom, is right here and right now." He's as comforting as his father, almost. Officer Escobedo circled us, taking photos of everything—me, the broken sidewalk, and so on.

The emergency squad expertly transferred me to a stretcher. Anita told them to take me to nearby Alhambra Hospital, thereby saving the day. Officer Escobedo followed to be sure I was all right, and took more photos.

Alhambra Hospital was new, handsome, and nearly empty. The E.R. was swarming with a U.N. of doctors, nurses, and orderlies. Nurse from China, doctor from India, x-ray tech from Hawaii. (Me: "I was born in Honolulu." He, unimpressed: "Me too.") Only three other patients in the whole place.

The E.R. was tastefully done, with lime walls and mauve curtains to match the mauve chairs. All of the equipment was sleek and new. This must be a hospital for billionaires, I thought. The bill will probably kill me, if I live that long.

I got the full treatment: brain x-ray, CT scan, tetanus shot (optional but "required at this hospital"). Toby and I waited for the test results. "What do you do for a cracked skull?" I murmured.

"Mom," he laughed, "you don't even have a headache."

A smiling Filipino aide suddenly appeared with gourmet lunch on tray (hot chicken soup, fresh pasta with delicious sauce, three juices—cranberry, grape, and apple—dessert of minced pear with whipped cream and angel cake).

1:30 P.M.: Diagnosis arrived. Nose broken, cranium uncracked. Praise the Lord. "Ice the swelling, take Tylenol for pain—aspirin keeps blood from clotting." Amazingly, I didn't have any pain but took Tylenol just in case.

2:30 P.M.: Discharged. As Toby wheeled me out, a gracious attendant asked me to sign papers. My eyes were so swollen Toby had to read them to me. "Good day, dear lady," the attendant bows. "You have been here as our guest."

If you need an emergency room, try to get to Alhambra Hospital in L.A. Only one complaint: they were not enough impressed that an eighty-seven-year-old fell flat on cement and didn't break any bones (nose doesn't count). But my cheering squad, Toby and Anita, were.

3:00 P.M.: Only one hour late (incredibly), we headed north in Toby and Anita's new van, me lying on the back seat foldout bed.

Happy to lie flat, I was shaken but okay—until I looked in the mirror. Two black eyes, the left swollen shut, huge goose egg on forehead (Toby: "Bumping out is better than bumping in."), swollen nose bright red and still oozing blood.

In that van-converted-to-ambulance, I met for the first time Manolo's beautiful bride-to-be, Michelle Gray from Australia. She took one look at my battered face and patted my hand sympathetically. It was the beginning of a true friendship.

Awash with thankfulness, I was determined to get to Thanksgiving dinner. My face looked like raw beefsteak, but Kate Hodgetts-Bisno, Melissa's niece and my adopted granddaughter, rigged me up in a wide-brimmed hat draped with a black lace veil. I could see out, but nobody could see in. I felt like Marlene Deitrich. I even managed to slip turkey beneath the veil, which took some doing. I explained my plight by reciting a famous limerick.

> For beauty I'm not a star
> There are others more lovely by far,
> But my face, I don't mind it,
> Because I'm behind it.
> It's the folks out front that I jar.

Confident that I'd had my disaster, I was more than ready to go home. At six A.M., five days after the accident, Toby drove me to Los Angeles Airport. Doctors had pronounced me fit for travel, and I was eager to head back to the barn. I could see out of my swollen black-and-blue eyes, but just barely. My broken nose, covered with two large scabs and painted red with mercurochrome, was a showstopper.

"Toby," I said, "don't you dare try to park. LAX is jampacked. I go by wheelchair, and the wheelchair people are expert at getting you on the plane."

As they say in Edwardian novels, "Little did I wot."

My wheelchair person, Annie, was overweight, sullen, and silent. Maybe she was scared by my face. It scared me. She parked me where I could see America West Flight 408. I said, "You'll come back and put me on the plane, right?" No answer. She seemed to have lost the power of speech. If she ever had it.

I read the paper, drank tea from my thermos, and waited. Later I looked up as she slumped by. "Annie," I called, "isn't it time to take me to the plane?" She sauntered over and pushed me to the gate. The ticket-taker said: "This plane is leaving. The gate is closed."

"It can't be, I can see the plane," I yelled. "It can't be leaving."

"The gate is closed, lady. There is nothing I can do."

My voice rose many decibels. "Get me on that plane," I shouted. "I *have* to get to Boston."

An America West official who heard me (as did everyone else) ran over. "Can I help you?"

"I want to talk to the boss."

"I am the boss."

"Get me on my plane, RIGHT AWAY . . . please."

"I'm sorry, madam. Once the gate is closed, there's nothing I can do."

"What do you mean?" I demanded. "I can see the plane, just sitting there."

"I wish I could stop it. There's nothing anyone can do." Wheelchair Annie stood beside him, looking blank. I was probably her first passenger. I bet I was her last, too.

To sit in a wheelchair and see your plane leave is the definition of agony. "Is this an airline or a torture chamber?" I shouted. "My bags are on that plane—my pills are in them. I need those pills." Boss didn't say, "Why don't you carry them in your purse?" He called my daughter, Cissa, in Boston, who blessed him out. I have to admit the poor man kept his cool.

This was not my finest hour. Unlike Kipling, I do not equate triumph with disaster. But his poem "If" flashed into mind, thanks to the memorizing we all had to do when I was young. Kipling is good for all seasons. "If you can keep your head when all about you/Are losing theirs and blaming it on you . . . you'll be a Man my son." The other ending came to mind: ". . . then you don't understand the situation."

Boss confers with his cell phone. "The best I can do is send you to Las Vegas in an hour. You'd change planes there—a two-hour wait for the plane to Boston. You'll arrive four hours later than you planned."

I drew myself up and announced: "I am eighty-seven years old and I do NOT change planes."

He tried to switch the subject. "Didn't you hear them announce your plane?"

"I'm deaf. I wear two hearing aids but I still can't understand those announcers."

That did it. The combination of my battle-scarred face and towering anger wiped him out. "I've worked here two years and this is the first mistake I've made," he said limply.

I fumed all the way to Vegas (of course I changed planes). I got my first and last view of Sin City, a burned-out desert punctuated with blue swimming pools. Like Ruth, I was in alien corn. Three thousand miles from my beloved New Hampshire, I couldn't even speak Vegas.

A second boss met me and danced attendance. "We've talked to your son in Boston," he said. "Your luggage will be delivered to him." While I waited, still fuming, America West's crisis manager fetched food, drink, newspapers, magazines, anything I wanted. What I wanted was to be in Boston with my luggage.

It isn't just by chance that my kids call me the Unguided Missile. For a few minutes I toyed with staying over in Vegas: a chance to fatten my purse? Impress my friends? Meet new guys?

When I finally arrived at Logan, four hours late, Tad was right there waiting. As I was wheeled toward him I exclaimed, "Tad, you look like the Rock of Gibraltar." He laughed, "Mom, in that wheelchair you look like a guided missile."

Notes to my two literary heroes: Dear E. B. White, I had my disaster and I've written it up. Now I'm waiting for the money to roll in.

Dear Ned, do misadventures count?

Belly Dancer Visits Old Folks' Home

I buy into the cliché that young people keep you young. Leyla Ka-malick, Dartmouth Class of 2002, is my proof. Tom and I met Leyla when she showed up at St. Thomas Episcopal Church, a pea-green freshman from Texas. I needed a writing assistant and Tom said, "Any Dartmouth kid who volunteers to teach Sunday School is reliable. Hire her."

He was a good picker. In four years Leyla was never late, never missed a day. She won a fellowship to teach creative writ-ing at Phillips Academy, Andover, and loved teaching but found prep school a bit stuffy. "I read Snake Hips *by Anne Thomas Soffee, a Lebanese American who finds fulfillment in belly danc-ing. I was drawn to that subculture, a world of women from all walks of life, celebrating their non-stylish bodies. One must have a belly to belly dance.*

"My grandmother is Palestinian American," Leyla added. "All Arab women belly dance." Leyla had invited me to her final dance recital, but it was too far. "All right," she said, "I'll bring my recital to you."

❦

You Are Invited to
A Belly Dancing Party
Featuring the Famed
Arabian Bellyist
Leyla Kamalick
Harvest Hill   3:30 P.M.

Reactions varied. Surprise: "Belly dancing? Are you kidding, or is this for real?" Curious: "How old is the belly dancer?" Academic: "Is that a word, bellyist?" Outrageous: "Is it true a belly dancer can write her name with a piece of chalk in her navel?" (Answer censored.)

Carried away by the thought of belly dancing in my apartment, I invited a few friends. Fifteen gathered in my living room. They ranged from seven-year-old Safyia Hill Walker to ninety-four-year-old Mounir Sa'adah, a Harvest Hill resident who emigrated to the United States in 1945 from Beirut. "In my day," he said, "belly dancing wasn't for polite society. But men liked to watch it and pin money on the dancers."

When Leyla walked in, she gasped. "I wasn't expecting an audience." Feeling only slightly guilty, I said, "Belly dancers attract people." She laughed. "Where shall I dress?"

While she changed, Mounir spoke to us about Oriental dance. In the Middle East the expression "belly dancing" is never used. That scandalous name was invented for the Chicago World's Fair of 1890 to draw a crowd, which it did. Middle Easterners consider it a vulgar term for a beautiful performing art.

Oriental dance did not, as most people think, originate as a dance of seduction done by concubines. In the beginning it was a fertility folk dance performed by men only. Later, at single-sex gatherings, women took turns getting up and dancing for each other. (This was one way mothers of marriageable sons could evaluate eligible young women.) Even now some orthodox Muslim women won't dance where men other than their husbands can see them. By and large, though, Oriental dancing is something Muslims of all ages do when they gather for joyous occasions, especially weddings.

Mounir ended with a flourish: "Men write poetry, women *are* poetry." (My feminist friend Dr. Proctor rolled her eyes.)

The Bellyist walked slowly in and bowed. Was this our jeans-wearing, hardworking Sunday school teacher and Dartmouth Phi Bete? Mata Hari came to mind. Leyla, gold earrings dangling, bells on jeweled belt tinkling, gold toe-rings shining on bare feet, was scantily clad. The translucent maroon chiffon costume sparkled, a hip-hugger that revealed a bare belly. Her brief maroon top, edged in rhinestones, dangled pearls over fair skin. Two slits up the sides of the ankle-length skirt were highlighted by beading. Leyla's large green eyes, rimmed in black á la raccoon, sparkled, but her smile was muted.

Her friend Leigh flipped a switch and sensuous Arabic music started with a slow beat. Smiling enigmatically, Leyla began to undulate, clicking her gold castanets. In each hand she held her sheer black veil, edged with sparkles, which she wove back and forth in ever larger circles. The skirt swayed; her thick hair grazed her shoulders; the intensity of the music increased, as did her hip figure-eight's. It was controlled ecstasy.

Leyla's three seductive dances took half an hour. The audience was mesmerized. There is nothing, but nothing, like belly dancing to zing up an afternoon at an old folks' home. Watching Leyla dance would rejuvenate Methuselah.

The F-Word

1909. My brother Red was seven. One day our Victorian mother heard her little boy swear. Horrified, she washed his mouth with soap, sent him to his room, and called the post chaplain.

Chaplain Easterbrook didn't mince words. "Do you know what happens to little boys who swear, Red? When they die the devil sticks a sizzling pitchfork into them and roasts them over a slow fire. Then he dips them in a vat of oil and pitches them into the fire." Red jumped to his feet and shouted, "That sonofabitch!"

1947. Tommy was five. One day I heard him use a bad word. "Get into the car, Tommy." We drove to the park for privacy. I stopped the car. I said, "Tommy, did I hear you use a bad word?" He nodded. "You must promise me never to say that word, ever again." He promised. We had a serious talk about taking God's name in vain, kissed, and made up.

That night, I described Tommy's transgression. His father exclaimed, "My little boy said 'God damn it to hell'? Damn it, I can't believe that."

With aging, the name of the game is adjustment. Not easy. Consider the f-word. Nothing is more upsetting to my generation than the constant repetition of the f-word. It is repeated ad nauseam in movies, books, plays, grammar schools, playgrounds. *The New York Times* and I may be the only ones left who still use blanks. Everybody else fills them in.

I shudder every time I hear it. Let's give the f-word a well-earned rest. After all, it has been working overtime since it first appeared in Middle English (1100–1500).

Tom and I were shocked when the f-word was first used at our dinner table. It was a dinner party in 1953. Harold Taylor, president of Sarah Lawrence College, was describing a White House reception he and his wife, Muriel, had attended. "Ahead of us in line was Duke Ellington. When he reached President Eisenhower, the Duke kissed him on both cheeks." Harold paused dramatically. "Ike didn't know whether he was fucking or flying." I laughed, but not really. What if the children heard him?

Even I was indignant, however, when Rinehart published Norman Mailer's war novel *The Naked and the Dead* and substituted the phony word "fug." Tallulah Bankhead, meeting Mailer for the first time, said: "So you're the young man who can't spell fuck."

Our friend Leonard Kent, who enlisted in the army three days after graduating from Harvard, told me, "It was World War II that outed the f-word. We could not have won the war without it and SNAFU—'Situation Normal: All Fucked Up.'"

Clifford Procter, ex-naval officer, agrees. "During the war the f-word spread like a virus," he told me. "One gob who had the temerity to ask his chief bo'sun why they were re-painting the foredeck got this polysyllabic tottering house-of-cards reply: 'You guys is gonna paint this fucking deck ir-re-fucking-gard-less.'"

For me, language hit a new low when Vice-President Dick Cheney used that rotten word on the floor of the U. S. Senate to curse Patrick Leahy, the distinguished senator from Vermont. Sickening. I felt like J. D. Salinger's Holden Caulfield, who protectively erased 'fuck you' from a men's room wall.

The first time I saw the dread word in print was in Florence in 1939. I bought a contraband copy of *Lady Chatterley's Lover* and sat up all night reading it. The next day I felt sick amidst the dizzying marble of the Medici Chapel and had to go back to bed.

Perhaps the vice-president who jolted the country should have tried Mark Twain's solution: self-censorship. In *Life on the Mississippi* Twain says, "You blankety-blank-blank." Leaving something to the imagination would be refreshing.

Fast forward to 2005. "Have you a copy of *On Bullshit?*" I asked.

"*What?*" The clerk was startled.

I repeated loudly: "*ON BULLSHIT.*" People turned to stare at me.

I may not be able to say the f-word, but being specific about a book title isn't hard. Of course, at my age, bullshit does not come trippingly off the tongue. But that is the name of a book by Princeton Professor of Philosophy Emeritus Harry G. Frankfurt.

This slight little book, which my brainy friend James describes as "intense inquiries into the mundane," is the best example, ever, of the power of a book title. It hit number four on *The New York Times*'s non-fiction bestseller list, beating out Pope John Paul, Johnny Damon, and the South Beach Diet. *The Times* delicately listed it as *On Bull——*.

It turns out that the professor wrote his bestseller twenty years ago. It was a thoughtful essay examining the difference between bullshit (which he related to humbug) and lying in our moral culture. Widely read by scholars, the essay was ignored by everybody else.

Then one day Ian Malcolm, the director of Princeton University Press, had a genius of an idea. He gave the essay its resounding title and published it as a pocket-sized hardback book, sixty-seven pages bound in linen and handsomely printed with the wide margins you never see anymore.

Professor Frankfurt scored a hit. He was invited to appear

on the *Today Show* and Jon Stewart's *Daily Show*. But not because of his book's philosophical ruminations. Who would have guessed that a book title could pack such a wallop?

My husband and I used to play a game called "What's Your Favorite Title?" Tom's was *Treasure Island;* mine, *Great Expectations.* He said RLS knew *Treasure Island* would make even a dolt pick up the book. I said Dickens put his finger on every parent's tender spot with *Great Expectations.* We both agreed on the best non-fiction title: *No Place to Hide,* by our friend David Bradley. It was a powerful warning of the danger of radiation, based on horrors Dr. Bradley found in the Bikini Islands after the atomic tests had been conducted there. *The New Yorker* published most of it.

Tom liked titles that have become part of the language: *How to Win Friends and Influence People, You Can't Go Home Again,* and *Everything You Need to Know about Sex but Were Afraid to Ask.* I prefer titles with a literary aura: *For Whom the Bell Tolls* (John Donne); *The Sound and the Fury* (Shakespeare); *Absalom, Absalom* (Bible); and *Splendor in the Grass* (Wordsworth).

I'll skip the List of Worst Titles, mentioning only in passing *God's Politics* and *The Raw and the Cooked.* According to the internet, the front-runner for great book titles is *Elvis Is Dead and I Don't Feel So Good Myself* (not for my generation).

Bennett Cerf, the fabled editor and creator of Random House, said adding the words "how to" will turn any book into a bestseller. Asked about *Gone with the Wind,* the runaway bestseller of his day, Cerf, who never gave an inch, replied, "They would sell a lot more copies if they called it *How to Gone with the Wind.*"

Some titles have a life of their own. My kids grew up on *Chitty Chitty Bang Bang,* which later took on a new life as a hit musical. A title like that draws the young like a magnet.

Some titles are peculiar but enduring. *Catcher in the Rye* has been a must-read for teenagers for over fifty years. The text is the voice of a teenager, but the title sounds like Yogi Berra on whiskey.

Some titles grab you but give away too much, like *Death in the Afternoon.* In Hemingway's tale you can be pretty sure that someone isn't going to be home for dinner. And with Fitzgerald's *This Side of Paradise,* you sense that someone else is going to miss dinner, for a lot more appealing reason.

Endurance, Victory, and *The Agony and the Ecstasy* suffer from too much testosterone. Try a little estrogen, guys. Or at least a Valium. *Little Women* and *Little Men,* on the other hand, ensure avoidance by young jocks.

You've got to hand it to Booker T. Washington. *Up from Slavery* gets a lot of mileage out of three words. *Portrait of the Artist as a Young Man*—great book, but the title invites mockery. Dylan Thomas, for instance, entitled his life story *Portrait of the Artist as a Young Dog.*

I wish Tom were here to enjoy the *On Bullshit* title brouhaha. He would have loved it. The text may be slow, but the book is moving fast. And I find it makes a splash when the old lady's gift turns out to be a book she delicately calls *On Bull-poop.*

Sex Talk

The film Kinsey *took us back to the forties and fifties, when the word sex caused high anxiety. For the born-yesterdays, Dr. Alfred Kinsey, a Harvard-trained zoologist at Indiana University, shook up my generation. The first person to research sex scientifically, he wanted to find out, "What do people actually* do *sexually?" So did most of us, although not for the sake of science. His 1948 bestseller* Sexual Behavior in the Human Male *empowered us to talk openly about sex.*

But people my age are still hesitant.

Ads for *Kinsey* said: "You'll be shocked at how far we haven't come." Well, I for one have come a long, long way. Leaving the movie, I said to Laurel Stavis, the young friend who took me, "That was strong stuff."

"Really? How so?" I almost tumbled into the generation gap between us.

"I'm not used to movies that measure penises and count orgasms."

"Did it bother you?"

I hesitated. I wasn't sure how I felt about the frankest movie I'd ever seen. Suddenly it came clear. "No. It's high time Americans admit sex is basic. It should not be hush-hush as it was in my day. We didn't know the correct word for anything."

Laurel laughed. "Amazing."

I grew up in the Age of Innocence. Sex was a mystery to be solved by marriage. My mother, born in 1879, was reprimanded for saying "Mrs. Jones is expecting." To cop Johnny Carson's quip, not even a pause could be described as pregnant.

John Dewey taught my generation to learn by doing, and we did the best we could. But I wasn't the only one holding onto modesty. I once sent an article called "Fifty Years of Sex" to *The New York Times Magazine. The Times* bought it but deleted my story about the five-year-old spilling coffee in her grandmother's lap and lisping, "Gwanny, did you burn your wagina?"

I was indignant, but editor Jim Greenfield spoke with authority. "The word vagina has never appeared in *The New York Times,*" he said, "and it never will." The year was 1989.

I've come a long way, and so has *The New York Times.* Recently they ran an article on "vaginal rejuvenation," whatever that is. They also quoted a female college student: "A year ago I wouldn't be caught dead with a condom, but now it's like a credit card—you can't leave home without it." When I was in college I'd never seen a condom, and I thought oral sex meant talking a good game.

It's impossible to keep up with the changing mores. Today the threat of AIDS has colleges handing out safe sex kits. As surgeon general, Dr. C. Everett Koop issued 107 million pamphlets on AIDS. I applaud Dr Koop, but one sentence shook me: "Dating does not mean the same thing as having sex." No one had to tell us that.

My husband and I were in our thirties and had three children when Alfred Kinsey's book shattered taboos, giving us the vocabulary and the courage to discuss sex in detail. Nobody would believe how uninformed we were.

Now Dr. Kinsey is hailed for advancing human knowledge;

then he was hounded by the media and the moralists. Kinsey infuriated them by maintaining that so-called sex education had always been "morality disguised as fact."

In the end, a congressional committee investigated Kinsey's work. As a result, the Rockefeller Foundation, which had so bravely financed him, canceled all his support. As the movie makes heartbreakingly clear, Kinsey then fell into a deep depression. The actor Liam Neeson (one reviewer called him "a sequoia of sex") was unforgettable. His Kinsey was driven, difficult, brilliant, and, in the end, unbalanced. Two years after congress investigated him, Dr. Alfred Kinsey died of a heart attack. He was sixty-two.

Kinsey began our liberation and then the pill changed all the rules. How does an old lady sort it all out? I cheer for the sexual revolution that needed to happen. Surely it was a mistake for the wellspring of life to be unmentionable, or mentioned only in what were then called dirty jokes. I take it as a sign of health that today anything can be and *is* discussed. Enlightenment took a long time. I doubt we'll ever return to the so-called "morality" I grew up with.

Although people age, I've been happy to discover that emotions do not. After fifty-nine years of marriage, my husband still delighted me sexually, albeit with a difference. I've been a widow for five years—but the memory lingers on. Kinsey transformed sex into an open book. But love remains a mystery.

Fortunately.

Deep Talk over Tea

Tom and I began our married life communicating intensely about movies, books, food—everything except what matters. Life does not let you live in a cocoon. For fifty-nine years we struggled to say what we felt. Along the way we had a lot of professional help, but the biggest help was necessity. As the years dwindled down to a precious few, we knew we had to communicate before it was too late. I'm still thinking of things I wish I'd said.

"Thank God for tea! What would the world do without tea? How did it exist? I am glad I was not born before tea." — SYDNEY SMITH, 1771–1845

I like to ask friends, "What's your idea of a good time?" Their answers are revealing, ranging from "babysitting my grand-daughter" to "shopping when I have lots of cash" to "eighteen holes when my putter is hot."

My answer, arrived at late in life, is deep communication with another human being. I take my cue from my hero Anne Morrow Lindbergh, who wrote, "The most exciting thing in life is communication." It is not easy to come by.

I used to think alcohol would do it; now I know tea is better—and you can remember the conversation. Walking is also good. My kids say running together works, but my legs won't take it. And how can you talk when you're winded? Talking over tea cups beats all.

By trial and error, over more years than you can even imagine, I made up my Rules for Communication.

1. A cup of hot tea is a mysterious enabler.

2. Two people is the limit. "Tea for two and two for tea / Me for you, and you for me." Invite someone who doesn't want to discuss weather, health, or neighbors.

3. The Art of Listening is essential. This is hard. As my years increase, so does my urge to talk all the time.

4. Interruptions not allowed—switch off phone, radio, TV, and cell. (Easy for my age; impossible for the young.)

5. Silences are welcome. All therapists know this. To get a person to open up (and that includes me) takes time and patience.

"There are few hours in life," Henry James wrote in *A Portrait of a Lady,* "more agreeable than the hour dedicated to the ceremony known as afternoon tea." In my day, tea parties were the thing: some small, some large (hats and short white gloves). But that's not what Henry James and I are talking about. Tea parties produce chatter, not communication.

Asians, who build beautiful tea houses in quiet gardens, know that the setting influences conversation. Two chairs side by side facing an open fire are good. Two fireside chairs facing each other are better, as long as they are close together. Distance may lend enchantment but it's death to communication. A big gap between chairs is a Communication Preventer.

Above all, tea demands leisure time. As a Chinese proverb says, "A hasty man drinks tea with a fork." Mr. Yip, a Tea Master who owns Jabbok Tea Shop in Hong Kong, explained to a reporter, "Tea has been important to Chinese life for over 3,000 years. It brings out the concept of harmony, which is the central theme of Chinese civilization. Tea can be a real linkage in relationships."

A Chinese student told me about the Tea Club, a traditional two-story Chinese tea house in Beijing where the elaborate ritual of tea drinking takes place in leisure and privacy, a privilege that costs $6,500 a year. The Japanese tea ceremony, on the other hand, is elaborate and incomprehensible.

In hot weather, tea on a porch or in a garden works fine—unless you have black flies or chatty neighbors. Iced tea is all right, but not for me. Hot tea, "the cup that cheers but does not inebriate," is what keeps me going, winter and summer.

My Perfect Time-Tested Cup of Tea: Preheat teapot with boiling water. Empty. Then add one tea bag per person, plus one for the pot. Pour boiling water slowly over tea bags (never add tea bags to water). Warning: I found out the hard way that letting tea bags steep for more than five minutes robs the flavor. It also looks terrible.

The hotness of everything matters to me. I prize my fifty-year-old tea cozy, which will keep a pot of tea hot until kingdom come. Important: on your tea tray, don't forget a jug of boiling water to dilute tea as preferred; also, small sugar cubes, cream (not cold), and lemon slices with a clove in each.

True tea snobs use only loose tea in an earthenware teapot—but I think tea bags are fine, unless my guest is English. The British loathe "the little American mouse on a string." After I wrote a column about my travel disasters, I got a card from Vi and Ned Coffin in Vermont. "Eleanor Roosevelt said, 'A woman is like a tea bag. You can never tell how strong she is until you put her into hot water.'"

Bagged or loose, the kind of tea matters. I like Earl Grey best. Lapsang Souchong's smoky flavor is not good at breakfast time but excellent at tea time. If you prefer herbal tea, you're on your own. The older I get, the more I appreciate caffeine, but not in coffee. Coffee stimulates, tea soothes.

What we drink our tea out of matters to us tea snobs too.

Bone-china tea cups are traditional, but too small for serious tea drinkers. I prefer preheated glass mugs. I've never had a cup of tea that was too hot. Large mugs won't do at all. Before you finish, the tea is cold.

In this country, it is impossible to get a cup of hot tea at a hotel or restaurant. You are expected to select a tea bag and then dunk it in lukewarm water. Terrible. I wait till I get home. Even those expensive, chic coffee houses seem to fear pouring boiling water over tea bags.

When Tom entered Harvard in 1934, President and Mrs. Conant invited the freshmen to their home for Sunday afternoon tea. It was a glorious day and only Tom and one other freshman showed up. Tom's mother was a tea lover, but it must have been a first for the other student. "Cream or lemon?" Mrs. Conant asked. He was stumped. He hesitated a long time, then, beaming, announced: "Both."

I detest high tea. The most famous example is at the Victoria Hotel in British Columbia, which requires a reservation and is really supper. Fine if you're starving, but not if you want to communicate. Tea should be kept simple. Robert Frost liked to take raw eggs with his tea, but most of us prefer something less original. Cinnamon toast is best, and perhaps very thin cookies. If you must have sandwiches, in my book there are only two kinds for tea. You can have cucumber *or* watercress or you can have cucumber *and* watercress.

Tea and anything just sounds inviting. The phrase "Tea and Sympathy," now part of the language, was the title of Robert Anderson's 1953 hit play (later a Deborah Kerr film) about the problems faced by a sensitive prep school boy accused of homosexuality. He's "saved" by the headmaster's wife. (Here, sympathy means sex.)

When Tom was courting me (as people used to say in our day), he took me to high tea at the Palm Court of the Plaza

Hotel. String quartet, flowers everywhere, way too many sand-wiches and cakes. Zero communication. It was like watching a movie. A month later the two of us tramped through the Sanc-tuary (Andover's nature preserve) and had one-on-one tea with cinnamon toast in a cabin at the summit. We talked about what was important to us (Tom: friends and graduate school; me: writing and Mozart; both: books and laughter).

Yes, Anne Morrow Lindbergh said it all. "The most excit-ing thing in life is communication."

For all these recipes, I use Pepperidge Farm thin-sliced white bread. Be sure to cut off the crusts.

CINNAMON TOAST:
Spread bread with soft butter, cover with cinnamon sugar, and bake until crisp. Warning: cinnamon sugar burns easily.

CUCUMBER SANDWICHES:
    Hellman's mayo, thinned with lemon juice
    One cucumber, peeled and sliced very thin
    Finely chopped onion (scant)
Spread mayo on both slices. Add cucumber with a bit of onion. Season to taste with salt and pepper. Cut sandwiches into four triangles.

WATERCRESS SANDWICHES:
Flatten crustless bread with rolling pin. Spread with soft cream cheese. Season. Cover with watercress. Roll tightly. Cut in half. A few leaves should stick out the end (very enticing).

The Pursuit of Happiness

My hobby is commencements. They are like a maternity ward: everybody is keyed up and smiling.

Over many years I've attended countless commencements and enjoyed most of them. The most unforgettable advice I ever heard came from television's Mr. Rogers. He told the students about a hundred-yard dash in the Special Olympics. One of the nine racers fell, hurting his knee. The others did not race on; they all came back to help him. "What really matters," Rogers said, "is helping others win, too, even if it means slowing down and changing our course."

The quintessential commencement speaker was Robert Frost. He put his forty honorary degree hoods to good use—he had them made into a quilt. I heard him speak at three colleges—Wellesley, Sarah Lawrence, and Dartmouth. One of his poems, about a "stormy, stormy world . . . And the sun's brilliant ball," seems to me to invoke a rainbow. It is titled: "Happiness Makes Up in Height for What It Lacks in Length."

Erika Knight, Lebanon High School valedictorian, came up with one of the most original ideas I have heard at a commencement. Quoting her grandfather, Bishop W. Earl Ledder, Erika said, "It's not the pursuit of happiness that is important, but the happiness of the pursuit."

Flashback, 1952: I am sitting in the kitchen of our house on Paradise Road in Bronxville, licking (remember stamp licking?) S&H green stamps and fitting them into the squares of an S&H booklet. In walks my mother, visiting from Virginia. "What are you saving up for?" she asks.

"A Waring blender. Then I'll be able to make delicious soup out of leftovers and quick Hollandaise."

Mine was the kind of mother who spent her life trying to make sure that her children got everything they wanted. She would say, defensively, "My four children won't take spoiling." (Her secret weapon: a disciplinarian husband.)

Later the same week my mother brought me a gift. I exclaimed, "Thank you—I love surprises." I unwrapped it quickly and my heart sank. It was a brand-new Waring blender. I tried to hide my disappointment; of course it was irrational. I could use my stamp books for something else, but the happiness of the pursuit had vanished.

I'm told this same psychology applies in business. The pursuit of your first million is exciting. After that, ho hum. I wouldn't know; I don't do money. But I know from experience that the happiness of pursuit applies to Easter Egg hunts, treasure hunts, and Christmas Eve.

My grandson Ned, when he was at Union College, told me, "Road trips are usually more fun than the destination." The Cunard line agrees with Ned: "Getting there is half the fun." Which brings us back to the old conundrum, which is better, anticipation or realization? The poet said, "Ah, but a man's reach should exceed his grasp / Or what's a heaven for?" (Ten points each for poet and century.)

My husband and I had a running argument about which was better, anticipation or realization. I voted for anticipation, Tom for realization. The discussion came up whenever we took a trip. I'd guess the final score was fifty-fifty. One of the facts about being the surviving partner is that you find yourself continuing old conversations. I banter with Tom regularly— and win a lot more often than I used to.

On a highly anticipated Elderhostel trip, I could hardly wait to get to Scotland, land of my ancestors. Scotland was even better than its pictures, but the food in the universities where we stayed was so meager and tasteless we finally took to pub dining. On the other hand, when we went "climbing" in Switzerland—we got as high as the first stop on the Matterhorn trail—the Swiss Alps were beyond anticipation: pure white at dawn, rosy at sunset, lavender by moonlight. I'm still replaying them in my mind's eye.

The ultimate pleasure-of-pursuit song is "I'm Forever Chasing Rainbows" (melody stolen from Chopin). I also collect rainbows. My southern mother said they foretell good luck. I record each rainbow in a notebook, with date, place, and description. Either I've been remiss or rainbows are less frequent than they used to be, probably because we abuse the environment.

My earliest rainbow is dated April 1969, Bronxville, New York: "Partial—unable to see pot of gold at either end." One of my best sightings is from May 1975, Amherst, Massachusetts: "Caught brilliant rainbow reflected in a puddle. Symbolic?"

My most recent and most exciting entry is from August 22, 2005, 7:00 P.M., Lebanon, New Hampshire: "Perfect double rainbow, with large band of blue sky between the two. Never expected to see anything like it. I felt like Noah after the flood. A double rainbow must double your luck."

In our memory course at Harvest Hill, we relearned the rainbow acronym "Roy G. Biv." My writing assistant, Beth—who is wonderfully observant—jumped out of her car to look at the double display. She told me that the inner double rainbow went from purple to red and the other reversed that, going from red to purple. Beth is accurate, a problem I've never had.

What I want to know is who is responsible for those reliable colors appearing from nowhere? Not what causes rainbows—any science student can explain that. But what causes those causes? Or, as my little granddaughter Iris once asked, "Who puts up the rainbow, Grandma?"

I, too, would have stopped my car and jumped out to look, if I hadn't sold my car and stopped driving forever. The two rainbows filled me with delight mixed with awe, then mixed with nostalgia for the rainbow-lover I married.

Another flashback, Upper St. Regis Lake in the Adirondacks, August 1950. Our second son, Tad, age five, has caught his first fish. Standing barefoot on the dock, waving a bamboo pole with a six-inch perch hooked on a string, he is yelling, "Go get somebody! Go get somebody!"

"Go get somebody!" is the perfect reaction to a dream suddenly realized. The older we get, the more most of us relish nature's wonders. I looked at the double rainbow and ran to get my fellow nature-lover, Frances Field. She was already out on her balcony, gasping in excitement. Fran ran to tell the bingo players nearby, who said, "Oh. Next number?"

Glorying in the otherworldly display that lit up the evening sky, I blessed my high school English teacher, who made us memorize this, among many poems:

> My heart leaps up when I behold
> A rainbow in the sky.
> So was it when my life began;
> So is it now I am a man,
> So be it when I shall grow old,
>   Or let me die!
> (Ten points each for poet and for his two centuries.)

When the poet said "man," I'm sure he was talking generic, not gender. Oh well, enough of quizzes, here are the answers: "On Reach," Robert Browning, 1812–1889; "On Rainbow," William Wordsworth, 1770–1850.

Geriatric Dating

Widows are by definition loners. After Tom died in 2000, my friends rallied round and took me out. They know how much I miss him. They also know that I want to see everything. As time went on, I would buy extra tickets and invite people to join me. But that was costly. I don't mind going to the movies by myself, but concerts and lectures are different. Just as the need for companionship began to bother me, one friend invited me to an interesting lunch.

§

The friend who introduced us said, "James is a widower and lonely."

"I can identify with that," I said.

She took me to lunch with two other friends (female, bespoke). James turned out to be a physicist, tall and thin and intelligent. He had spent his youth working his way around the world. Eventually, he settled down, got two degrees at MIT, and landed a job on the Manhattan Project.

On our first date he invited me to a play at the Northern Stage in White River Junction, Vermont, a Sunday matinee. I was taking my walk on Saturday when suddenly there he was. "James," I exclaimed, "our date is tomorrow!"

"*Really?* I have the wrong day? I've never done that before."

"Think nothing of it. I get days mixed up all the time. It's one of the joys of aging." I'm older than he is, so I was enjoying his mix-up.

He likes to walk, so he joined me for my mile and we talked politics. We are both devoted to the same party, which helped. I said, "I'll meet you at the theater tomorrow at one-thirty. The matinee starts at two." I got to the theater promptly at one-thirty and he was there, all right. He and nobody else.

"The play doesn't start until five o' clock," he said. We both laughed, a good sign.

What to do for three hours?

We drove back to my apartment at Harvest Hill. "You go in the study and read *The Sunday Times*," I told him. "I'll go in my bedroom and take my nap." That kind of date suited both of us. I had a good rest and he absorbed the book review. He's a book person and that's good, too.

Later we both enjoyed the play and a Chinese dinner afterward. I sent him an e-mail: "Dear John, Thanks for a good time."

He e-mailed back: "You can call me John if you like, but I'm used to James." Ah, me.

Next we tried a movie date. We went to see Jack Nicholson in *Something's Gotta Give*. After ten minutes James said, "This is terrible."

We got up and left. Walking down the corridor we passed the movie *Mona Lisa Smile*. "Let's go in. I'd like to see that." I was enjoying Hollywood's silly idea of college girls and the beautiful Wellesley campus when James said, "This is terrible. Let's go."

In the car I said, "You're hard to please. I think you must be hungry."

"I am."

We went to an Italian restaurant in Lebanon: closed. We drove to a Thai restaurant in Hanover: closed. All-American place: overflowing with parents and screaming children. Ended up at a hole-in-the-wall. Food: terrible. Conversation: forced.

After this downer of a date, I took heart from a remark I heard Mike Nichols toss off on TV. "Cheer up, life isn't everything."

The next day I e-mailed James: "You set a new record: two movies and four restaurants in half an hour. What is your idea of a good show? *Long Day's Journey into Night?*"

His reply: "Yes, O'Neill. Also Sophocles, Aeschylus, and Aristophanes."

I e-mailed: "You're a literary snob. Maybe we can agree on Charlie Chaplin and Katharine Hepburn?"

Looking back over his e-mails, I see that, in writing if not in person, James isn't above a little blarney.

Last March: "I still have some $$$ after taxes, so keep a lookout on the entertainment front. I need tax relief." We went to a ballet and enjoyed ourselves—and even each other.

After the fender-bender that made me give up driving: "Reading your article was a huge relief and pleasure. Nobody who wasn't in top condition could write that well. Amazing how you can turn tragedy into good writing . . . and so soon."

After the publication of my book: "At Thanksgiving, my son the doctor mentioned that he had started and was enjoying your new book. When I got home I got out *Everyday Matters* just to remind me what he was reading about. Big mistake! I kept going, and going, and . . . "

While visiting with his son in California: "My son said I should ask you to come visit us at his hideaway in the hills for two weeks. I thought the best I could expect is a day or two. Now, after your travel nightmares, I'm more doubtful. (You must promise not to fall off the cliff, it's a long way down.) What think you?"

I replied, "I stay well if I stay put."

After a long silence: "I sent two e-mails and haven't heard from you. Are you not getting my e-mails? If you don't get this one, notify me immediately. If you do get it, notify me even faster."

When James returned from California, I invited him to lunch at Harvest Hill. I told him I'd meet him at the front door. "No," he said. "I'll come to your apartment first."

"Fine," I said. I waited at the front door of the dining room. He waited at my apartment. A half-hour passed. He deduced the solution and appeared at the front door. I was sorry I was the one who got mixed up this time.

They say that with real estate there are only three considerations, "location, location, location." It's the same with geriatric dating. Rule number one: never ever change location.

Both of us love the Connecticut River. On a beautiful July 4th, James and I took two camp chairs and a picnic to the town's boat landing. He brought the sandwiches and I brought the iced-tea-plus-lemonade and cookies.

I was glad I didn't bring those sandwiches. When James bit into his, he said, "Uh-oh." He put his hand to his mouth and spit out a tooth. Previously cemented in, it had suddenly let go.

My empathy overflowed. The month before I had lost a tooth at breakfast—mine must have just crumbled, because I never retrieved it. I had to get a boughten one cemented in. In the annals of aging, losing a tooth comes second on my Horror List. Number one is losing a hearing aid. Enough said.

I asked James to read my version of geriatric dating and give me his opinion. His answer: "It's okay, but don't use my name."

"Don't worry," I replied. "I can't remember it."

Go Ahead and Take the Risk

We brought our children up on Dr. Seuss. The great wit, who graduated from Dartmouth in 1925, had words of wisdom for every situation. One of my favorites is You're Only Old Once! A Book for Obsolete Children. *I like being called an obsolete child, because that's how I feel. When I was a child I had to ask permission for everything. Now there's nobody to ask, so I turn to Dr. Seuss, and he gives me a green light.*

> You have brains in your head.
> You have feet in your shoes.
> You can steer yourself
> any direction you choose.
> — DR. SEUSS

"You can steer yourself any direction you choose." Good advice for graduates but questionable for eighty-somethings, most of whom, like me, need a helper. Yet when my young Mississippi nephew, Charles Reeder, age sixty-two, offered to take me to France, I hesitated. Knowing I longed to make a pilgrimage to Normandy beach and to Mont St. Michel, he offered to be my helper. Should I go? *Could* I?

It's scary to take a leap. Looking back, I wish I'd taken more of them. I wish I had accepted my chance for a master's degree fellowship at Wellesley. Why did I continue teaching high school

English instead? I was afraid, that's why. I just didn't think I could do it.

Suddenly I had a flashback (I live in Flashbackland). My husband, deep in a biography of Robert Frost, was saying, "Listen to this. Frost says, 'The people I want to hear about are the people who take risks.' Isn't that great?"

"I dunno—why take a risk if you don't have to?"

Tom, whose confidence was as unobtrusive as it was solid, said, "Why not? That's what risks are for, the taking."

I called Charles Reeder and accepted his offer. After all, he was really the one taking the risk. I said, "Promise me if I drop dead you won't tote my body home. Just bury me on the spot, okay?"

"You won't drop, Aunt Nardi," he laughed. "You're made of tough stuff."

"So are you, Charles."

We both wanted to visit the Normandy beach where my brother—his uncle—Colonel Red Reeder, landed sixty years ago. And Charles knew I had yearned to go to Mont St. Michel since I was ten. On the gold cover of my favorite childhood book was Mont St. Michel, with the ocean swirling around its small island and its spire touching heaven. To me it looked like Camelot, where knights were gallant and ladies fair. I was heavily under the influence of a novel called *When Knighthood Was in Flower*.

Four days before we left, half of the new $890 million Air France terminal at De Gaulle, where we were headed, collapsed, killing five people. Talk about risks. But we never saw the wreckage. Passengers were herded into a bus and driven endlessly around to get to another baggage area.

Taking a taxi to our small suburban *relais,* we drove through the tunnel where Diana was killed. The location is marked with a "Gold Flame" presented by the United States. Like everyone else, I had wept for the star-crossed princess. High speed is a risk not to take.

Charles let me choose what we'd do with our three days in Paris. "The most beautiful city in the world" is heady stuff. Number one was a return to St. Chapelle, the thirteenth-century "chapel without walls" built by Louis IX. I had been mesmerized by it in the summer of 1939. That was my first trip to Europe—not on my Virginia teacher's salary of sixty-nine dollars a month, but on a huge (to me) bank loan. Come to think of it, that was a big risk—for the bank.

Once again I sat in the stained-glass silence and dreamed of Henry Pentagenant of England (Laurence Olivier) being crowned King of France here, after he vanquished the mighty French at the Battle of Agincourt.

I had to see architect I. M. Pei's crystal pyramid entrance to the Louvre, once a risk, now revered, but we skipped the Louvre itself (too crowded). I wanted to return to the Rodin Museum, which had bowled me over when I first saw it. Sixty-five years later the voluptuous, erotic statues were even more powerful, because I thought I knew what Auguste Rodin had in mind.

Seemingly, Paris had not changed since Tom took me there in 1950, except that there were no *pissoires*. Charles and I tried to recapture that golden time. We sipped café au lait in dappled sidewalk cafés, ate crepes at *creperies,* and talked about the meaning of life (how French). We strolled the Left Bank of the Seine, trying not to buy anything (how un-American). It wasn't hard. A postcard cost two dollars, and the *International Herald Tribune,* ditto.

Charles rented a Renault, and with his old friend Jacqueline Le Prince as our mega-coordinator we drove through bucolic Normandy, where cows and sheep dotted green meadows. The French were celebrating the sixtieth anniversary of the greatest invasion in history, and they gave us a warm welcome. Unlike more recent conflicts, World War II had a crystal-clear purpose, an easily defined enemy, and liberators who were greeted with open arms. When a Frenchman rear-ended us at a red light in Normandy, our French friend ran back, yelling, "You get out and apologize to your liberators."

Near the famed American Cemetery a billboard says: "Golf—Omaha Beach, eighteen holes." Each hole is named for a famous general. Off-putting but touching, too.

Of the 150,000 Allied soldiers who landed on June 6, 1944, 3,000 were slaughtered in the first two days. The perfectly-groomed cemetery ("CEMENT-ery") is beyond awesome. Endless rows of pure white crosses on emerald grass, colonnades and reflecting pools, rose gardens, American flags, and beyond, the blue Atlantic. The bodies of 9,300 lie buried here (55 percent of the bodies were sent home by request). Most moving to me: the Wall of the Missing, with its pitiful little bouquets.

Charles said quietly, "Let's have an Unk meditation." Jacqueline found a small empty beach, code named Gold, where the British had landed. We sat on the sand and read aloud Red's letter to my grandson, seven-year-old Peter Campion, who had asked, "What did you do on D-day, Unk?" What Red did was lead 3,000 men ashore on Utah Beach and into lethal combat until—on D-Day plus six—his leg was shattered by a German shell. Red's letter concluded, "When you are there, Peter, climb the sand dunes and look inland. Try to visualize the huge lake the Germans made to keep us out and our Twelfth Infantrymen wading through it to fight and win."

From Normandy we headed to Mont St. Michel. When I had seen the Cathedral of Notre Dame, recently de-sooted and now a dazzling white, I thought I had died and gone to heaven. But when I realized my girlhood dream, Mont St. Michel, I *was* in heaven. How did medieval man get those huge stones up into the sky? (Our English-challenged guide: "Lots of bloody.") The Abbey fortress, begun in 1020 and finished five hundred years later, was protected by ocean tides but is now approached by causeway. Mont St. Michel, with its gothic spire reaching into the heavens, is inspiring beyond the telling of it.

I was determined to climb to the top, no matter what. The narrow winding streets of the little village are always jammed with tourists, but as we climbed, the people disappeared. Through archways, up and up, the steps got wider, until we reached the Grand Staircase. I heard a guide say, "A lot of people have died here. Can you think of a better place?" I could.

By the end of the climb, two French women were pulling me and Charles was pushing, but I made it to the Cloister at the top. We gazed out at the known medieval world and wished the tides would rush in as they used to. Charles said, "I'm glad the spire is closed, otherwise you'd want us to climb that."

Leaving Paris was like parting with a lover. Aboard the plane, I asked the steward if I could move to a window so I could see Paris from the air. The gallant steward bowed and moved me into first class. The gourmet dinner on that plane equaled any French restaurant in the United States. Poor Charles ate his heart out in coach.

Flying home, overstimulated, overfed, and overwhelmed, I tried to thank Charles and ran aground. "I was intimidated when you offered to take me to Paris and Normandy . . . "

"Aunt Nardi," Charles interrupted, "you must have forgotten what Granny said."

What my mother, a born gambler, had said when she was dying is family legend: "I don't go in for regrets. The few regrets I have are the chances I didn't take."

Words failed me. I just squeezed his hand.

How Did I Get Here?

Everyone has formative experiences; the trick is to learn from them. From the vantage point of eighty-plus, perforce learning is easier.

The attentive reader will glean the following lessons from these chosen memories: vanity, vanity, all is vanity; a treasure is a treasure is a treasure; when in doubt, opt for the new opportunity; when still in doubt, hire a hypnotist; and, cancer isn't the end.

I Was Always a Loser

I'd like to blame my talent for losing things on aging, but alas, no. I have been gifted at losing since I was six, when my brand new white bucks disappeared, never to be found. To combat my problem, I strive not to be a things person. At the top of my Don't Want List are jewels.

One Christmas dinner years ago, we played "What Is Your Favorite Possession?" Tom said Koko, our olden-golden retriever. Tommy said his motorcycle; Cissa, her piano; Russell, his new driver; Tad, the education he didn't have to pay for (he won a Rhodes Scholarship to Oxford). Toby put us all to shame—he said his wedding ring.

On our fifty-seventh wedding anniversary I had to revise my "non-things" pose. Tom surprised me with a string of real pearls. I love them almost as much as I did him.

I opened the gray velvet box to reveal the creamy, glowing strand on white satin and fell into a chair. Tom said I had earned them. No way. But I accepted the gift and the accolade *con brio.*

The card was less romantic. "See *The Scarlet Letter,* chapter six." I pulled Hawthorne's masterpiece off the shelf. Tom's reference made me laugh out loud. Hester Prynne had "named the infant Pearl, as being of great price, purchased with all she had."

Uneasy lays the head that wears the pearls. Right away I started worrying about my pearls. Are they safe? Is the clasp secure? Maybe I should put them in the bank for safekeeping? But I was brought up to believe beautiful things should be enjoyed, so when I flew to Mississippi to see my beloved brother, Fred, old and ill, I took my pearls to show him.

I thought about wearing them for safety. Does one wear jewels on an airplane? What if an airport thief yanked them off my neck? I've heard professional thieves don't steal pearls because it is bad luck. Is that true? Robbers grab gold chains off people all the time in New York subways. Gently, I placed the gray velvet box into my carry-on bag. I kept it with me at all times.

When I boarded a little air link plane in Memphis to fly to Laurel, the flight attendant, a young kid in white shirt and black shorts, said: "Your carry-on bag is too big to fit under our seats. I'll put it in the overhead." That seemed reasonable. But I felt edgy with my prized possession out of sight.

I still felt queasy when our puddle-jumper landed. "Where is my bag?" I asked.

Young kid smiled innocently. "All carry-ons are on the ground next to the ladder, ma'am." Creaking, I climbed down the ladder. No bag.

"WHERE IS MY BAG?" I shouted over the prop noise, trying not to panic. "INSIDE," she shouted.

Inside, no bag. Frantic, I ran to the desk. "Where is my carry-on bag?" I demanded. "That little girl on the plane took it away from me and now it's gone."

The fellow whose shirt read Michael said flatly, "It's still in Memphis."

"It can't be. I was holding that bag on my lap when they locked the plane door in Memphis." Later I found out that Michael's answer to everything was "It's still in Memphis."

Michael said smoothly, "Your bag must have been too big for the overhead, so the hostess put it in the rear with the luggage. Now it's gone back to Memphis. I'll call them."

He called Memphis. I waited, beside myself with anxiety. Nephew Charles, there to meet me, felt my pain, but what could he do?

Michael returned looking concerned, not worried. I was worried (understatement). What would I tell Husband? "Describe your bag," said Michael. "Can you point to a picture on this sheet that looks like it?"

"None of them look like it." My voice rose dangerously. "It was just a carry-on shoulder bag with a zipper."

"What color?"

"Blueish; well, greenish. Blueish greenish. It's a copy of a Monet painting."

"A *what?*"

"It's a picture of a garden in the rain."

"Was your name on your bag?"

"No." Now we both knew I was a saphead.

Charles tried to soothe me. Fred's only child is a story in himself: Princeton Class of 1962, University of Mississippi LLD, married Ole Miss Beauty Queen, Zen Buddhism student in Japan, full-time meditator, divorced. New life: happily remarried, practicing Episcopalian, devoted father of four, and full-time golfer. His Mississippi accent is impenetrable; his sense of humor infectious.

Michael returned from the phone. "Is there something in your bag to identify it?"

I try to recall one identifiable thing. I'm certainly not going to tell him my priceless pearls are in that bag. "Yes, there's a blue plastic folder marked 'Wellesley College.'"

"Wesley College?"

Charles whispered, "You're not in New England anymore." I just nodded, feeling sick. I wished I'd never left New England.

Michael relayed the dubious information to Memphis and returned. "They'll find it. I think."

Now I really was a wreck. I had disappeared my beautiful new pearl necklace. Charles said, "Remember Granny's mantra when she lost something: 'They were only *things*'?" My mother's mantra does not work for me.

Charles the lawyer took up my case. "Michael," he drawled, "the plane stopped in Meridian. Why don't you call them?"

Michael dialed, talked into the phone. Listened. Came back all smiles. "They have it. They unloaded your carry-on with the other bags in Meridian."

Weak with relief, I gasped, "How soon can I get it?"

"They'll send it on the next plane, due in at eight tonight."

Frantic, again, I said for the umpteenth time, "I have to have that bag. Can you get it to me in Laurel tonight?"

"Sorry, ma'am, you'll have to wait until morning."

"Can't you send it by taxi?"

"There are no taxis, ma'am. We're in the country. I'll send it as early as possible tomorrow."

My lawyer weighed in, polite but firm. "Michael," Charles drawled, "this is Northwest's mistake, pure and simple. I am sure you can figure out some way to get that bag to my aunt tonight."

Michael's cool was beginning to melt. "I'll do my best, sir. Give me your address and phone number, ma'am, and I'll see what I can do. We use Hotshot Express."

"Hotshot Express," I muttered. "You bet."

Charles said, "And you give me the name and number of the person who will be at this desk in the morning."

"Sylvia comes in at five A.M. Here's her number. Sylvia will take care of everything." Michael was oozing confidence. I oozed defeat.

Shell-shocked, I collapsed in my nephew's car. We hadn't gone far before I asked, "Is my suitcase in the car?" Charles made a U turn and we returned to the airport. The luggage place was locked up tight. Charles located someone who knew someone who had a key.

All that night I tossed and fumed. How was I going to tell the hideous news to my dear, sweet, generous, logical, cause-and-effect, use-your-head husband?

I waited until 5:30 A.M. to phone the airport. Sylvia answered. "I'm calling about my carry-on bag."

"What carry-on bag?"

"The one they put off by mistake in Meridian."

"I don't know anything about that," said Sylvia. "Sorry." She sounded testy.

I shouted, "You know Michael, don't you?"

"Yes."

"Michael said you'd help me. What am I going to do? I have to have that bag. I'm desperate. This is a crisis."

"Excuse me, ma'am, this is news to me. Can I call you back?"

"No. You'll wake up everybody. Don't call me, I'll call you." I stewed for half an hour, then dialed the airport.

Butter wouldn't melt in Sylvia's mouth. "Good news, ma'am! We found your bag in Meridian. It will be at your house by 7:15 this morning." I stifled the urge to say, "I bet."

7:15 came and went. 7:30. 8:30. No Hotshot Express. No bag. No nothing. I tried telling myself it's just M.T., Mississippi Time, but my stomach churned dangerously. At 9:00 A.M. the doorbell rang. A smiling driver, maybe nine years old, handed me my Monet bag and departed.

Hands shaking, I unzipped the bag and felt around inside. I touched the gray velvet box. Pulled it out and there, lying on the white satin, cool and virginal, were my pearls-sans-price. I put them on and—after I stopped shaking—vowed *never* to take them off.

The pearls Tom gave me to celebrate our fifty-seven years together are only *things*, Mama? No way.

How to Buy a New Bathing Suit

As the wrinkles have increased, my wardrobe has changed. I never wear shorts or sleeveless blouses in public, let alone a bathing suit. I keep my terry robe on until I walk into the water. I then hand it to my daughter and she scurries it back to shore.

When my geriatric date James invited me to go swimming at a nearby pond, I declined. Many years ago, when Tom and I were young, comparatively speaking, I worried about my bathing suit; these days I worry about my birthday suit.

Beware of all enterprises that require new clothes.

— HENRY DAVID THOREAU

"Will this do?"

"Do what?"

"Do to wear to the pool bash, of course."

Tom and I had been invited to a posh pool party, not a help-us-clean-off-the-leaves kind, but turquoise water and lush towels. I was trying on my bathing suit.

"Having a child for your old age doesn't do much for your figure," I added bravely.

Long silence. Then, ever tactful, Tom said, "You bought that B.R.—before Russell—didn't you?"

I couldn't remember when I bought it. I did recall wearing

it in a sapphire lake surrounded by snowy peaks in Switzerland. I couldn't understand why everyone was staring at me. Then a little girl came up and asked, "Lady, why are you swimming in a dress?"

I caught Tom's drift and shuddered. For me, buying a new bathing suit is roughly equivalent to swallowing castor oil or rolling in poison ivy. Year after year, I cling to the bathing suit I have, postponing the dread day when I must shop for another.

"All right then," I said crossly, "I'll buy a new bathing suit." I felt like Huckleberry Finn when he declared, "All right then, I'll free Jim and go to hell."

"I'll drive you, if that would help," Tom offered. I knew his presence would be as helpful as a case of Saint Vitus's dance. My husband loathed shopping. Just wear what you've got, was his motto. But his smile melted my hard heart. "That would help a lot," I lied.

On a breezy day in May we set out on the Bathing Suit Quest. Tom was feeling good. "I'll foot the bill," he said. "The sky's the limit." Driving through the spring green and thinking bathing suit, he said, "Do you remember when the Ransoms used to have three subscriptions to *Playboy?*"

"Yes. I thought it excessive."

"Not at all. Six sons equals two boys per issue. I guess poor Papa had to wait his turn."

I could see how Tom's mind was running. This wasn't going to be easy. He pulled up in front of our most expensive store and patted my knee. "Let's do this right."

The elegant shop displayed heavy sweaters, wool skirts, winter coats, and a chic collection of skiwear. "Where do we look for bathing suits?" Tom asked innocently.

"*Bathing suits?*" The saleswoman rolled her eyes upward. "They won't be in until February."

Tom was indignant. "Whatever happened to this summer? It hasn't even begun."

"Perhaps, sir," she said, "you should try the mall."

The mall did have bathing suits—piled on an end-of-the-season sale table. How dumb of us to think May was the beginning of summer. Tom settled on a stool to read his paper. "Find one you like, never mind the cost."

I pawed through the shiny satin suits and the slippery rayon suits looking for my size. They were all made for six-year-olds. I finally uncovered an orange and pink elastic horror. Although it was marked size twelve, I struggled into it with great difficulty. It seemed to be some kind of super girdle.

I consulted Husband. A mistake. "I don't get it," he said thoughtfully. "How could a woman who plays tennis and avoids sweets and starches look six months pregnant?" No words came. I glared.

We left the mall and drove to the plaza. The shops in the plaza think they are grand. The clerk at the first store handed me a one-piece, multicolored rayon handkerchief. "What is this?" I asked.

"A *maillot*." She spoke as if she were suffocating with boredom. I held the *maillot* in front of me and looked in the mirror. "Interesting," Tom said. "That will show your belly button. Belly buttons are in, very sexy."

"Why don't you go sit down?"

The suit was sliced away to expose both hip joints. "Is there a skirt to go with this skimpy thing?" I asked. "I don't need this much of me showing."

The saleswoman shrugged and sauntered off. So much for the *maillot*.

The next shop we visited had a few silky tank suits my size in neon shades of hot pink and electric blue.

"Do you have a suit with a built-in bra?" I asked.

The salesgirl's eyes widened. "*Bra?*" She pronounced the word as though it were Swahili. "Nobody wears a *bra.*"

Tom grinned. "A woman after my own heart."

"Why don't you wait in the car." Not a question.

He got up. "I think I'll wait in the car."

Two stores later I did unearth a bathing suit with a built-in bra. Tom was still taking an interest. I held it up and he studied it. "It seems to be constructed of reinforced concrete," he said slowly, "with two Howitzer emplacements."

Bravely I struggled into the bulgy thing. This time when I looked in the mirror I shrieked. Tom said, "You look like Big Bosom Bertha at the circus."

"Oh, shut up," I snapped. He did, for a while.

The next shop was having a bathing suit sale. A bikini sale, that is. "This is more like it," Tom grinned. The bottoms were swatches held together by thongs across the hips. "No need to try one on," I said. "With my bulges, I wouldn't even see the bottom half." His silence was worse than the wisecracks.

I closed my eyes and pictured the bathing suits of my youth. In Panama, my mother made me a stunning suit out of an Indian print bedspread. It had a halter neck and I thought I was the cat's meow. Unfortunately, she lined it with flour sacking to insure modesty. It was like swimming in an overcoat. We won't even mention the white rubber suit that split wide open when the fleet was in, back in Panama during my heady teenage days.

By now my spirit was broken. Not Tom's. "Where next?" I collapsed in the car, leaned back and closed my eyes. He looked at me and turned sympathetic. Patting my hand, he said, "I'm sorry I needled you."

Without opening my eyes, I said, "I'm sorry I told you to shut up."

"Why don't we try Dan and Whit's?" he suggested.

Dragging myself into Norwich's old-fashioned, we-carry-everything store, I muttered, "This is my last gasp."

"Hooray," he said.

Sure enough, they did have a few one-piece suits made of flowered cretonne. I held one up. Miles too big. What bliss! A bathing suit could be too big for me. I tried on the smallest one. Tom said, "You look like you're wearing a lampshade." I put the suit back and bought two packs of green rickrack.

The next day, when he came home from work, Tom found me bent over my sewing. This in itself was news. I saved all of my sewing to do when I sat up at night to watch catastrophes, like earthquakes or presidential elections.

"Sewing?" he exclaimed. "Has some disaster struck?" He pointed to the yards of wavy tape. "What's all the green stuff?"

"That," I said firmly, "is kelly-green rickrack. I am using it to trim my navy bathing suit. Borders of green rickrack will jazz up the old suit. When I wear it to the pool party, women my age will say, 'Wherever did you find that suit? I've been looking for one just like it.'"

Tom chuckled. "You remind me of the old saw 'The ladies of Boston do not buy their hats. They have them.'"

Three Nights on the Connecticut

Tom and I first met Dartmouth Professor Noel Perrin via our mutual friend Dick Ketchum, editor and founder of Country Journal, *shortly after we moved to Hanover in 1977. Ned took us to lunch and we laughed our way through it. "I'd like to blow up all of the bridges that cross the Connecticut," he told us. Was he kidding? I'm still not sure.*

After I wrote about our canoe trip down the Connecticut River, I gave it to Ned to edit. His verdict: "Seventeen pages is too long. The Times *will never use it." He was right, of course. Eventually, thanks to Ned's help,* The Times *travel section did publish "Three Days on the Connecticut." Ned was always right about writing.*

He soon became my full-time editor. What larks! (That's Ned quoting Dickens, "Wot larks, eh, Pip old chap?") Unlike most editors, Ned was quick, often giving me his comments the next day. He read every word, knew which were wrong, right, or missing. And he always edited with wit.

Tom observed mildly, "You're becoming Ned dependent."

"I certainly am," I said. "Isn't it wonderful?" I'm not sure he thought it was wonderful, at first. But Tom became as devoted to Ned as I was. For twenty-five years, right up until the last two months of his life, Ned edited everything I wrote, always making it better, never accepting credit.

Ned Perrin taught me to write short, to write in pictures, and to focus on my last paragraph. I never thought my next-to-last paragraph would say that our dear friend Ned Perrin died on

November 21, 2004, after a heroic battle with a hateful form of Parkinson's called Shi-Dregger.

Our long, intimate relationship gives the lie to the old maxim: "True friendship cannot exist between a man and a woman." Ned Perrin was my best friend. I will miss him forever.

‽

There is nothing—absolutely nothing—half so much worth doing as simply messing about in boats.

> —Ratty from *The Wind in the Willows* by Kenneth Grahame

When I suggested a three-day, fifty-nine-mile canoe trip on the Connecticut River, Tom laughed. "At sixty-five? When was the last time you were in a canoe? Sleep on a riverbank in the rain and fight bugs? No way."

"You don't get it. We're on the river during the day, but at night we'll stay at three different inns. Our luggage will be waiting when we arrive each evening. We'll have hot baths and cocktails and gourmet dinners with wine and comfortable beds. I'm talking luxury canoeing, downstream."

"You can't count on luxury weather," Tom said. But he liked to try new things. He said he'd go.

Four friends agreed to go with us: Blair Winter, petite environmental researcher at Princeton; Gibson Winter, Tom's Harvard classmate, described in *Time* magazine as a "theologue"; Flo Mleczko, natural athlete, boundless energy, relaxed attitude; Ned Perrin, tall, thin, non-athletic, an author, farmer, and wit.

None of us had canoed recently. When Flo asked Ned if he'd brought his own canoe, he said, "Yes. I've always meant to take it out." Tom had the most experience. As a teenager at Camp Keewaydin, he spent summers paddling through Canada.

Inn-to-inn canoeing was the brainchild of Art Sharkey, proprietor of the Stone House Inn in North Thetford, Vermont. Our two other stops would be the Inwood Manor in East Barnet and the Atkinson House in Newbury.

On a rainy summer Monday, we gathered at Dartmouth's Ledyard Canoe Club, the oldest canoe club in America. "What the hell are we doing here?" muttered Tom, wiping rain off his glasses.

Art Sharkey said soothingly, "It's going to clear up tomorrow."

"Good!" exclaimed Gib Winter. We needed all the reassurance we could get.

We piled into a van that pulled our three canoes on a trailer and headed north. Our first stop, Inwood Manor, was simple— clean rooms, fresh white curtains, two bathrooms down the hall. "We have to be next to the bathroom," Blair announced. "I wouldn't let Gib bring his bathrobe."

It was too chilly to swim in the brook, as planned, so we decided on a long cocktail hour instead, only to discover that our inn did not have a liquor license. Tom located a not-nearby liquor store and stocked up. (In those days we were still drinking.) Too much wine, plus a driving rainstorm, did not make for a restful night.

Early the next morning, fortified by hot coffee, scrambled eggs, and bacon, we dragged our three canoes down a slippery bank to the Passumpsic River, which would carry us to the Connecticut, two miles away. The rain had stopped, but fog shrouded the trees and battalions of mosquitoes attacked our bare legs. Tom groaned. "I can't believe I paid money to be this miserable—and we haven't even started."

The Passumpsic widens as it joins the Connecticut and our boats began to move rapidly. "Osprey!" Tom called. A little later he discovered crows dive-bombing a great horned owl. "Some sight!" Things were picking up, birdwise. By the end of the trip Blair Winter, bird watcher extraordinaire, had spotted forty-eight different species.

Barnet's white-steepled church and green meadows, flecked with black-and-white Holsteins, came into view. Picture-postcard New England. Then Interstate 91 scarred the landscape and two trucks roared past. "I move we liquidate all trucks," Ned said. We rounded a bend and blissful silence descended.

We knew we had paddled seven miles when we heard the hydroelectric hum of McIndoes Dam, one of sixteen dams built to harness the power of the Connecticut. A sign said "Warning: No Boating Beyond This Point." Tom pointed to an arrow marked "Portage Trail."

"At every dam," Ned said, "we'll have a democratic vote whether to portage or go through the turbine."

"We only have two dams between here and Hanover," Gib said. "I looked it up." The men lugged the canoes, one at a time; the women toted the plastic bags full of food and gear. "I'm glad Gloria Steinem can't see us," Blair said. "Her motto is 'Don't send a boy to do a man's work, send a woman.'"

"Only four miles to Ryegate Dam, where we get to portage again," Ned said cheerfully, as we put our boats back in the river.

Tom and I had assumed we'd lead because our handmade boat was the lightest, but we were last, permanently. "What we have is a fat canoe," growled Tom, who always liked to be first.

The sun came out and reflections in the water doubled the purple loosestrife and black-eyed susans along the riverbank. "I can't tell where illusion ends and reality begins," I said.

"Like life," said Tom.

Then we seemed to go through a green tunnel—the banks were so high we couldn't see the countryside—until we passed an auto dump. Revolting. We'd been warned about Ryegate Dam: "The minute your boat speeds up, head for the shore." Suddenly, our canoes started to spin around, fast.

"PADDLE!" Tom shouted. We were dangerously near the falls. It felt like we were being sucked over. All of us paddled frantically toward Vermont. When we reached the west bank, we were panting, exhausted, speechless. Suddenly Ned announced, "We're on the wrong side. On the New Hampshire side, the portage is only fifty feet. Over here it's half a mile. We have to go back."

"Not on your tintype," growled Tom. "I won't risk going over those falls. We'll portage on this side if it takes all day."

It didn't take all day; it just seemed to. First, we couldn't find a place to land. Flo and Ned picked a spot with current zipping past. Tom called, "That's a terrible place. Too dangerous."

The current increased and I broke a cardinal rule: I paddled on the same side as Tom. Swoosh! Our canoe capsized and we both went under. I couldn't breathe. My heart pounded. I knew I was drowning. Terrified, I struggled to the surface— and my feet touched the ground. We were in shallow water. What a relief.

We could stand, but our canoe was swamped. I heard Ned's ironic voice. "I presume you did that on purpose."

"I'll get you, Perrin," spluttered Tom. His blithe spirit was almost quenched. He raised his voice. "Why in hell did you paddle on my side?"

"I got scared. We were headed for the falls. I thought we'd go over." He stared at me angrily. I stared back, timidly. Suddenly Tom laughed—then I laughed, relief flooding through me.

We both laughed so hard we could barely stagger to the shore. We hauled the plastic bags out of our boat. Our gear was still dry. The three men managed to lift up our canoe, dumping out a waterfall.

We thought we had retrieved everything; even Blair's borrowed bird glasses. "Damn it," Tom said, going through our stuff. "My sunglasses are gonzo." The sun was beating down and even a broad-brimmed hat wasn't enough. Flo gave him her extra pair. (Note to self: always take extra sunglasses.) Tom and I dried out quickly in the hot sun. But, alas, his beautiful Leica camera was finished. Kaput. Tom's reaction was unquotable.

By then it was two o'clock and we were starving. We sat on a log, six in a row, and gobbled our Inwood Manor lunch, molasses bread filled with ham and cheese. "What I wouldn't give for a cold beer," Tom said.

Back on the river, the wind had shifted to our backs, making whitewater rapids and whirlpools. We zoomed through a rocky gorge and came out on a wide expanse, as placid as a lake. "What determines the speed of the current?" I asked.

"Air conditioners," Tom replied. "If it's hot, everyone turns on air conditioners, the dams draw water to beef up the electricity, and the river runs faster."

"God has very little to do with river current these days," remarked the Theologue.

All day we'd had the Connecticut River to ourselves. Suddenly a Vermont voice called, "How's the watah?"

"Fine," Tom called back. "You have a great perch on that rock."

"Ayeh. We catch all the action."

Time passed slowly. Our bottoms were sore, our backs ached, and we had miles to go before we slept. Tom said, hands on back, "I need Toby the chiropractor."

"Who doesn't?" Ned said. "When Hester Prynne stood on the scaffolding, facing down her tormentors, Hawthorne wrote, 'It was one of those days she would pay for the rest of her life.'"

We were looking for our landmark, a red barn with a sign reading "Placey's Jersey Cattle Dairy Farm." We paddled on laboriously. At last the aroma of fresh manure floated over the water and Placey's farm came into view.

"Not much longer to go," Tom said innocently. What we didn't know was that we were in an oxbow, a loop-the-loop. You have to paddle five miles to end up a half mile from where you started.

Eventually, the red barn reappeared. Tom pointed to a stately elm overhanging the river. A sign hung from it: INN CANNOEA. "Cannoea?" I said

"That's the Latin plural for canoe, dumb-dumb," Tom said. "Pretty highbrow farmers."

We hauled our canoes up the bank, hid them in a field, and trudged a long, long way to Atkinson House. It's a retreat center for the United Church of Christ. One of the ministers had hung the learned sign to guide us.

As soon as possible, Tom broke out a bottle of dark rum. "Dr. Campion prescribes rum to get through the evening, that is, if you survive the day." That reminded Ned of Saint Nicholas, the model baby who refused the breast on Fridays because they were fasting days.

The next morning, as we prepared to leave the retreat center, we all sat in our canoes, waiting for Ned. "Where the hell is he?" growled my husband. At last Professor Perrin appeared, lugging his grandfather's beaten-up pigskin suitcase. He put it into his canoe, saying, "I don't want to be like Hemingway, who 'roughed it' in Africa while nineteen natives carried his gear."

Again it had rained all night, and gray clouds scudded before a stiff wind. "It's going to pour," I said gloomily.

"We can't get wetter than we did yesterday." Tom wasn't a Cheerie O'Leary; he just naturally felt things would turn out right. "How far to North Thetford?"

"Fifteen miles." Gib replied.

Tom beamed. "A piece of cake." Later we discovered Gib was talking highway miles, not river miles.

The sky lightened to powder blue and the sun broke through.

Tom got out his fishing rod. I paddled while he trolled from the stern. After we passed under the Haverhill bridge, Tom's line went taut. He thought it was caught on the bottom. No! A fish!

He played the fish but it did not tire. Just then six canoes appeared, filled with young campers. They stopped to watch Man Outwit Fish. Tom enjoyed the gallery. He told them he was using a gray ghost lure. Very skillfully he hauled in the fish and netted it. "A two-pound small-mouthed bass," he announced. The kids cheered and he bowed. I said, "Tom's a gallery player."

"All the best players are," said Ned. I scribbled in my notebook and one of the campers called, "Lady, do you have to write down every fish he catches?" Tom loved that.

We pulled up on a sandy beach to swim while Isaac Walton cleaned his fish. "The beginning of wisdom is when you start to carry a knife."

"Thoreau," said Ned.

"Mark Twain," Tom corrected him. "I like knowing something you don't know, Professor."

While we were "munchin' on nuncheon" (grapes, plums, potato chips), Ned recited part of Robert Frost's "New Hampshire":

> She's one of the two best states in the Union.
> Vermont's the other . . . And they lie like wedges,
> Thick end to thin end and thin end to thick end . . .
> One thick where one is thin and vice versa.
> New Hampshire raises the Connecticut
> In a trout hatchery near Canada
> But soon divides the river with Vermont.

Then he added, "Frost was wrong, of course. The two states don't divide the river. New Hampshire owns the whole thing."

"Did he know the facts, or didn't he care?" Flo asked.

"Frost knew everything," replied Ned, the true Vermonter. "His poem praising New Hampshire ends: 'At present I am living in Vermont.'"

Tom: "You have total recall."

Ned: "Yes, I remember the day I was conceived."

It was four P.M. when we reached Piermont. Tom called to an old fellow loafing on the bank, "How far to Thetford?"

"Thetford? Up here we classify our towns, fella. North Thetford, East Thetford, Thetford Center. You gotta be more definite."

"How many miles to North Thetford?"

"Ten rivah miles."

"Jesus," said the Reverend Winter.

"Maybe it's time to count our blessings," Tom said. "Wind at our back. Nobody has blisters. No bugs since the mosquito attack. No power boats. No other people. No daytime rain."

"And nobody has capsized since yesterday," Ned put in.

"Bald eagle!" Blair called in a low voice. A bird with an eight-foot wingspan wheeled over us and settled in a tree. Stealthily, we paddled toward the branch where our national symbol sat in splendor. He flew off, showing his white underwing marks. "Worth the whole trip," Gib said.

At long last we spied Orford's white steeple and green bridge. Ned, our floating Bartlett's, had a quote for the occasion. "Washington Irving wrote of Orford: 'In all my travels in this country and Europe, I have seen no village more beautiful.'"

We ached from sitting on small rawhide seats—and still had a long way to go. The sun dropped behind the blue hills. The river was pristine in the lovely evening light. There were a few clear bird whistles, then silence. "Magical," Tom whispered.

Church bells were striking eight when North Thetford loomed through the gloaming. Art Sharkey called from the dock, "You made it! Twenty-three miles in one day!"

"Feels like twenty-three hundred," I muttered.

The thirteen miles to Hanover the next day were a breeze. We pulled over to swim and loaf on the riverbank. When Tommy and Tad were at Dartmouth in the sixties, no one dared swim in the Connecticut. Raw sewage had turned it into a cesspool. Then Rachel Carson's *Silent Spring* sounded the alarm and, wonder of wonders, our government responded. Now we all enjoy its clear waters.

After our swim, we could hardly wait to get at Sharkey's picnic—chicken breasts, sliced avocados dipped in lime juice, apples and cheese. "I brought cold Chablis," Ned announced, to a round of applause. Pleasantly satisfied, we spread out in the sun while he read *Huckleberry Finn* aloud. "We slid into the river and had a swim . . . then we sat down on the sandy bottom . . . not a sound anywheres—perfectly still—just like the whole world was asleep . . . everything smiling in the sun, and the song birds just going it!"

Our trip ended back at the Ledyard Canoe Club in Hanover. A beaming Ned said, "I've discovered that paddling for three days is like building a stone wall. Your muscles hurt but your spirits soar."

My Christmas Hypnotist

*How can something as wonderful and magical as Christmas be
so stressful? Every year, no matter how hard I try to keep cool, I
find myself rushing to get last-minute gifts, Christmas paper,
and my cure for everything—more scotch tape. The year I realized that slowing down Christmas was a hopeless battle generated one of my family's favorite stories.*

I'm not fond of it.

❦

"Oh, Lord," I said, looking at the calendar. "Here comes
Christmas."

"As one grows older," Tom said, "Christmas comes every
six months."

December rolls round and everything goes on fast-forward.
There should be some way to slow down holiday speed-up.
But how? I wonder. Nothing seems to work. Once I got so
stressed out I even consulted a hypnotist.

Surprisingly, my energetic mother knew how to slow down
at Christmas. Instead of full speed ahead, she used to shift
gears, saying, "We have all the time there is." (You can't argue
with that.) When I was a child, she spent hours helping me
string cranberries and gild pinecones and make popcorn balls.
She even taught me to stitch red and green flannel into pen
wipers (who was wiping pens, I wonder?) and to glue Good
Humor sticks into trivets.

In December only, my mother used to bake Moldy Mice,
enough for everybody. If that took time, she never noticed.

(Moldy Mice: Preheat oven to 425. Cream together 1 stick soft butter, 1 cup flour, 3 tbsp. sugar, 1 tsp. vanilla. Place small lumps 2 inches apart on ungreased sheet. Top with crushed nuts. Bake 8–12 minutes. While still hot, coat with powdered sugar. Yield: 28 delicious mice—if you happen to enjoy eating mice.)

Every Christmas Tom would read *The Little Engine That Could* to our kids. "I think I can. I think I can. I think I can." That always prompted him to quote Henry Ford (not my favorite philosopher, but one of my favorite quotes): "Whether you believe you can do a thing or not, you are right."

Our early Christmases in Cincinnati weren't hectic. Easy does it was our mantra. The people we knew had time for carol sings and family gatherings. Tom and I had time to help the kids push hundreds of cloves into oranges to make aromatic pomander balls for gifts, which is saying something.

After our move to Bronxville, the pace speeded up. Rush, rush, rush. Hop the train for an eggnog party in town and pray you can catch a cab. Drive the kids to their cousins' in Long Island and fume in trafficlock on the bridge. Shop in jammed stores. Wrap packages at midnight. Write Christmas cards at the Cub Scout meeting. Bedlam.

Hurry-up was the name of the game. We were delighted when our neighbor Brendan Gill hurried over with a Christmas gift. What a nice surprise. We unwrapped the gold paper and found a bottle of Pouilly Fuisse, with a card attached that said: "Happy Birthday to Brendan from the Botsfords."

Speed is the enemy, and I'm not talking drugs. Our friend Eleanor Edelman once snatched up a tin of cookies and gave it to her niece. When the niece opened it she was delighted. Eleanor was aghast. Stored inside the tin was an heirloom silver dish. Ellie held her tongue but husband Albie never stopped kidding her. "Easy come, easy go, Eleanor."

Christmas, day of Peace and Love, could turn into a graveyard of great expectations. The long-anticipated checks from

Uncle Fred did not arrive. He crossed our boys off his list because they didn't write thank-you notes. Aunt Julia sent not the yearned-for cashmere sweater but scented shelf paper. Toby cried because Tad got more presents than he did. Cissa cried because she wanted the electric train Russell got. Tad cried because Tommy punched him. Once Russell, normally an amiable child, had a frustration tantrum—I can't remember why—and kicked over the tree. The crashing baubles and sizzling lights looked like test time at Alamagordo.

Then, before we knew it, our children were making Christmas in their own homes and we were unencumbered in our empty nest. You'd think we could finally embrace Thoreau's *Simplify, simplify.* Alas, no. "Every year," Tom told me, "you seem to get more frantic, rushing about looking for gifts, sending cards, wrapping packages. Slow motion gets you there faster, you know."

"Slow motion? What's that?"

I bought a book called *Unplug the Christmas Machine,* hoping it would help. It said children complain that "Mom is too uptight and busy." I didn't need a book to tell me that.

Eventually, even my mother sped up. I recall one Christmas morning in detail. Amid a cloud of red and green tissue paper, Mother is unwrapping a box with a picture of a pencil sharpener on it. "I always wanted a pencil sharpener," she laughs, "but not very much." Then she popped the unopened box into her present drawer to give someone else next Christmas.

True to her southern upbringing, she sat down and wrote her sister. My mother was honest by nature, with one exception: thank-you notes. She told Honey how happy she was to have the sharpener, what a joy it was to have pointed pencils, and so on. Honey replied by telephone. She could hardly talk, she was laughing so hard. "Open that box right away," she told her grateful sister, "before the cheese spoils."

The time I was really zonked by Santa Claus acceleration

was when Toby and Anita came from California for an October visit. She brought along my Christmas present. In *October*. No one is ready for Christmas then, except the stores and the people in TV commercials.

I stashed Anita's gift away carefully—I thought. I was in a hurry, naturally. But by the time December chaos set in, I could not find her package. "It's vanished from the face of the earth," I told Tom.

"Want to bet? It's here somewhere." Big help.

Years of experience produced my most valuable motto: "Don't look for anything. Buy another." How could I do that? I didn't know what it was. I searched until I felt sick, muttering, "I think I can, I think I can." There was no way I could tell Anita I had lost her Christmas present before I even opened it. Tom suggested, "Can't you just thank her without mentioning what it was?"

"No way. Anita's too smart. She'd know I was faking."

Tom, who was rereading Edgar Allen Poe, said, "Remember the Purloined Letter. It's probably in plain sight."

"I've looked in every possible spot, including plain sight."

Frantic, I remembered Patty Coughlin, who had hired a hypnotist to find a lost checkbook. The very thing! I called a hypnotist named Judy Magill, who was calm and reassuring. Of course she could help me. "In the mind," she explained, "nothing is ever lost. All we have to do is get you relaxed enough for the suppressed information to surface. Then we'll know where you put it."

"Just like a computer," Tom laughed. "Everything's on the hard drive, all you have to do is find it."

Judy turned out to be young and pink-cheeked. She looked like a soccer coach. She asked me to stare at a candle flame while she crooned softly, "All tension is leaving your body. You are getting drowsy. You are letting go . . . one, two, three . . . "

I drifted into a dream state, where I could still hear her voice but my limbs were too heavy to move. I was so relaxed I felt drugged. It was delicious.

When she brought me out of my trance, Hypnotist said, "You put that package away with great care because you love your daughter-in-law and you wanted to be sure you didn't lose it."

"I KNOW that," I shouted, tension flooding back like an electric current. "But where *is* the damned thing?"

Hypnotist remained cool and collected. "Maybe you will find it and maybe you won't," she said with a placid smile. "But I can tell you one thing. Your unconscious comments prove that you love your daughter-in-law and you know she loves you. Call Anita and tell her you lost her Christmas gift. She'll understand."

I kept looking for the present, but finally I made myself call Anita. Of course she understood. I felt wonderful and abandoned the search. That was worth paying the hypnotist her fifty dollars. As I discovered long ago, when you stop looking for something it's like going on vacation.

When the Christmas machine revved up again the next year, so did I. I grabbed a gift from my ever-ready present drawer (just like my mother's) to send our kids in California. It was a Japanese picnic kit, beautifully designed knives, forks, spoons, cutting board, corkscrew, in a sleek black case. It had turned up under our tree the previous year sans card. Handsome, but too fancy for our peanut butter picnics.

To my amazement, I got a call from Anita. "Can you get Tom on the phone?" she said. "Toby's on the other line."

We had a four-way hook-up. "We called to tell you," Anita began. She was laughing so hard she couldn't continue. Toby took over.

"Mom and Dad, you found it. The gift you sent us this year is the one Anita brought you last year. Merry Christmas!"

What I Learned in the Hospital

Aging leads to hospitalization as night follows the day. Anyone who experiences a good hospital is lucky indeed. I admit to prejudice in favor of Dartmouth Hitchcock Medical Center. Our son Tad is Dartmouth Medical School Class of 1971.

When I got a diagnosis of uterine cancer, Tom wanted to whisk me to that most famous eastern hospital, Mass General. He consulted Tad, who had been chief of geriatrics there but had since moved to the New England Journal of Medicine. *Tad's reply surprised us both: "DHMC is every bit as good as Mass General. Plus you'll be in a familiar place, among family and friends. That's worth a lot when you're sick. Stay where you are."*

I've always been grateful for Tad's advice. As Tom put it, "It's easy to underestimate local blessings."

Cancer. What a fear-full word. No one dared say it aloud when I was growing up. A diagnosis of cancer was a diagnosis of death. They called the dread disease "it," as in, "Should we tell her she has it? No, better not." By the time my cancer came along in the nineties, the word was still scary but most people could deal with it openly.

Our doctor, Linda Dacey, discovered the cancer cells in my uterus on a routine check-up. She scheduled my surgery as soon as possible. Tom said, "We've had lots of blessings, none more valuable than Linda."

The worst thing about my hysterectomy was kissing Tom good-bye when they wheeled me away. I could handle the operation; it was his look of woe that did me in. He held my hand until it was time to go.

When I came to, Old Faithful was right there. He leaned over and kissed me. "I love you," he said.

The surgeon came in. "Looks good."

"Doesn't she," Tom said, beaming.

"I'm talking about the cancer. We think we got it all, but you'd better have radiation, just to be sure."

"You're the doctor," Tom said. I nodded weakly.

I thought radiation would be simple. What did I know? I'd only had one other hospitalization (I don't count the blissful weeklong being-waited-on hospital visits when our kids were born). I had had an emergency gall bladder operation ten years before. All I remember now is how weak I was when they finally allowed me to get out of bed. Today they expect you to get up and walk out of the O.R., practically.

With my cancer operation I stayed at DHMC five days. "Whenever you're in a predicament," Tom always told the kids, "try to learn from it." During recovery I listed lessons learned "in hospital," as the Brits say.

DAY 1. The best medicine is a husband who enjoys reading aloud. Tom never tired of Thurber and E. B. White. Nor did I.

DAY 2. Having someone appear every time you push a button may be habit-forming. But if a nurse asks, "Would you like to . . . ?" say yes, no matter what it is. Otherwise, they never return—too busy. Whatever happened to nurses' crisp white uniforms and starched caps? A regrettable loss. (Whatever happened to starch?)

DAY 3. The U.S.A. is divided into five time zones: Eastern, Central, Mountain, Western, and Hospital Time. Of these, Hospital Time is best, that is, if you want time to stand still.

DAY 4. It is easier for a rich man to go through the eye of a needle than for a patient without a credit card to make a long distance call.

DAY 5. In a hospital there is neither day nor night, male nor female. It's all one. X-rays at midnight and modesty out the window. Hospitals are unisex. I wish my mother had lived to see the male nurses and female surgeons. She would have loved it— maybe.

I felt weak when I went home, but Tom had arranged for lots of help, which I needed. The radiation treatments were short and quick, and after each one I felt worse. I'm told it isn't a problem for most people, but for me radiation was a nightmare. My treatments tripped off a return of Montezuma's Revenge, which had first attacked me two years before in Mexico. Unfortunately, the radiation doctor was away at a conference and I got weaker and weaker. As soon as he returned, he stopped the treatments. But Montezuma didn't stop. After a miserable three weeks at home, I was eager to go back to the hospital. Anything would be an improvement. Our kids in Boston, Tad and Peggy and Cissa, took turns driving the five-hour round trip to care for their father, who was reeling with anxiety.

This time my treatment was intravenous feeding. Not one swallow of food or water permitted. I resumed my list of Lessons Learned.

DAY 6. Only a dodo says stomach when she means belly. In the gastroenterology world, *nothing* is of more interest than "Have you passed any gas?"

DAY 7. From a hospital bed, watching the changing light at dawn, any dawn—gray, snowy, or rosy-fingered—lifts the spirit. But there's precious little time for contemplation. Whoever thought of sticking a thermometer in your ear?

DAY 8. Few flower arrangements can equal a vase with a single rose bud that slowly unfolds. Get-well cards are relentlessly, hopelessly cheerful. None of them state the real case: Too bad you're sick. Rotten luck. Nasty break. Damn it to hell.

DAY 9. The best medicine is sitting in silence in the hospital chapel—even in bathrobe and attached to IV machinery—contemplating Sabra Field's stained-glass study of New England. It's all there, the snow, the frozen pond, the lights in the windows, the sunset glow, the stars sprinkled in a dark blue sky. (Yes, I know I have two best medicines. Actually, there are more.) If a prayer is wanted, Robert Louis Stevenson said it all: "Give us courage, gaiety, and the quiet mind."

DAY 10. My IV machine has a mind of its own. Machines will soon do everything; doctors will appear only to flip the switch. The Heroes of the Hospital are the geniuses who continually adjust and repair those critical machines, from monumental to minuscule.

DAY 11. If you're over fifty, a steady diet of television could drive you round the bend. Reading is a big effort. A transistor radio helps, as do books-on-tape and music tapes—especially music. Music hath charms to soothe the savage beast. Or is it breast? (Ten points for correct quote; ten more for the author.) If you want to lose your mind, watch TV after midnight. Wasteland is an understatement.

DAY 12. A note from a friend beats a visit because note reading requires little energy. (Whatever happened to visiting hours?)

If you're a patient, you'd better learn to love weather talk—it's even bigger inside a hospital than out. The best medicine is that rare visitor who gives a foot massage. Perfect bliss.

DAY 13. A scene on the wall you can gaze at can bring Zen-like calm. My picture, taped up by a previous patient, was Lake Louise—turquoise water beneath snowy peaks, soothing, mystical. As our Buddhist friend John Lincoln advised, "Don't just do something, sit there."

DAY 14. The best medicine is walking, even while pushing an IV rig. Forty times around two nursing stations makes a mile. (I never made it.) Or maybe the best medicine really *is* laughter. For that, I prescribe Father John Mullin S.J., Catholic chaplain at DHMC. "A doctor," he says, "is a fellow with inside information." John had a professor in seminary whose motto was "Love me, love my dogma."

DAY 15. A human being can get used to anything—in time. However, after eleven days with nothing to drink and no breakfast, no lunch, no dinner, the intravenously fed feels as if she's been reading Gertrude Stein—oh, for a little punctuation.

DAY 16. The best food you will ever eat is your first bowl of jello on your twelfth day of IV Living. But if you have to order your meals for an entire day at one swoop, your pencil is bigger than your stomach. Always.

DAY 17. The *best* best medicine is a husband who goes on reading aloud until he finishes the book, no matter how long it is. The book Tom kept on reading, *Personal History* by Katharine Graham, is a book for the ages. It contains much that is memorable, including this immortal sentence: "There is no greater wealth than health." *Amen.*

DAY 18. Make no mistake about it, nursing the sick is a great calling. And Dartmouth Hitchcock Medical Center is a great hospital—inspiring architecture, state-of-the-art technology, dedicated staff, talented physicians. How could I be so lucky?

DAY 19. A strong sense of your own mortality—hard to come by—clarifies your values.

The best medicine of all is husband, home, and family—oh, those dear, dear faces.

P.S. Answer to Day 11 questions: William Congreve (1670 – 1789), "Music hath charms to soothe the savage *breast.*"

People Met Along the Way

My mother was a people person; my father was a book person. Ergo, I must be fifty-fifty. If I were forced to choose, I'd come down on the side of people. As my friend Maizie Wilson (co-writer with Professor Arthur Wilson of *Diderot*) said: "I'm ninety years old and nothing that a human being can do will surprise me anymore."

And after all, isn't that the fun of aging, arriving via tsunamis and calm seas at a plateau of total acceptance? Looking back, I see now that much of my writing has been people-oriented.

The first article I ever sold was about Marty Maher, a fabled sergeant at West Point (*The New York Times Magazine*, February 19, 1950). I have published biographies of people who have fascinated me: Patrick Henry (leadership as eloquence); Kit Carson (adventurer into the unknown); Mother Ann Lee (founder of the Shakers, the "female Christ"); Connie Guion, M.D. Cornell 1917 (one of the first successful woman doctors, also a pioneer). My only venture into fiction was *Casa Means Home,* and that was based on a Puerto Rican boy whom I tutored in Harlem.

I think it's fun to ask people questions. I want to find out what they have done, or hope to do, with their lives and why. Here are some of the people that I have encountered over a span of too many years to count. One way or another, they are still my role models.

The Life of the Mind

Sooner or later life seems to throw everything at you. A few people are able to rise above the challenge. They are our teachers.

As I face the unknown, my teachers are the ones I meditate on—how did they do it? There are no answers. But we are given the example—and the Teachable Moments.

As my mother used to say, "All the best people are teachers."

The last thing I wanted to do was call on Clara Cohen Beiler. When I knew her in college she was brimming with vim and promise. How could I bear to see her paralyzed by disease?

As president of the Wellesley College Alumnae Association, I had gone to Cincinnati, where Clara lived, to speak at the Wellesley Club. I was having a good time until Harriet Chamberlain Wilson, my classmate and my conscience, looked me in the eye and said, "You're going to see Clara in the nursing home, of course." Of course. I hadn't seen her in years but I knew she was in grim shape. I was avoiding a visit. What a tragic error that would have been—for me. The impression she made that day is indelible.

Clara, daughter of a lawyer, had come to college from Great Neck High School in Long Island; I, daughter of a colonel, had come from Balboa High School in Panama. She was a brunette with lots of hair, a mellifluous voice, and a beguiling smile. From her happy-go-lucky manner you'd never guess she planned to be a serious poet. Though she was a freshman and I a senior, her insight could make me feel naive.

What we had in common was a benevolent dragon, Miss Elizabeth Manwaring, the formidable head of the English Department. Both of us were struggling to please Miss Manwaring, which Clara seemed to do fairly often.

After graduation I kept up with Clara through her brief entries in the class notes. Three years out of college, she married a research chemist. She wrote a joyous poem about the two of them "staying up all night, like secret lovers / to watch the Perseid meteor showers." Clara went to Columbia School of Social Work, had two sons, and cultivated her musical talent. She loved playing the piano in a chamber music ensemble and listed her occupation as "English teacher, social worker, director of research in a pharmaceutical company."

Her last entry, some years later, was heartbreaking: "Multiple sclerosis, age 45; divorced, age 55; occupation: invalid."

On that rainy Tuesday in Cincinnati I dragged myself to Beechwood Nursing Home. I knew Clara had been there four years. When I saw her I felt sick. She was lying utterly still in a darkened room. Paralyzed from the neck down, she could not move. A rush of empathy was nearly smothered by fear: what if that happened to me? How would I cope with helplessness?

Even talking was a challenge for Clara. She spoke through an amplifier that made her mellifluous voice sound tinny. "Nardi! How kind of you to come!" Clara's body might not function, but her mind did.

A short haircut made her look surprisingly young. I cast about for something to say. Did she still like poetry? "Oh yes, I compose in my head when I can't sleep. Writing in rhyme makes it easier to do the corrections. In the morning, I dictate my compositions to my nurse."

Unable to move but able to write poetry: almost a definition of valor. I felt like crying.

I stood at the foot of her bed and we talked about the old days. "Mr. Greene and Mr. Holmes gave me a lifelong passion for music," she said. She added with a rueful smile, still be-guiling, "I still go to the symphony."

"How do you do it?"

"They take me on a stretcher. Music is my bliss. My other salvation is books on tape. I'm a medieval freak. I'm reading *A Distant Mirror* on this voice-activated machine. Right now the bubonic plague is devastating fourteenth-century Europe. Barbara Tuchman on the Black Death makes me count my blessings." Silence. Then she slowly said, "We think we're in control of our lives, but we aren't."

I didn't know that the best thing I could have done for Clara was to keep her talking about the topic we all avoid: death. How I wish I'd said, "Tell me how you feel about the end of life, Clara. I try not to think about it." Instead, embarrassed by having touched a nerve, I changed the subject. "Tell me about your blessings."

"Lying here day after day," she said, voice stronger, "I know that my greatest blessing is Wellesley College. My education means everything to me." Another pause. "The life of the mind counts, you know."

I was deeply moved. But at the same time I wanted to get out of there. It was too much. Then, when it was time to say good-bye, I didn't want to leave. I had never encountered such an indomitable being. Nor am I likely to again. I had hoped to lift her spirit but she lifted mine. Clara had shown me, once and for all, that a human being can cope with any-thing. Anything.

Her mother had Clara's sixty poems privately published. Years later she sent me a copy. One verse says it all.

> Here moveless on the bed I lie
> Composing letters in my head
> With that in me that will not die
> Though all the rest is still and stiff and dead.

Clara Beiler pursued the life of the mind, her body "still and stiff and dead," five more years. All told, she had coped with multiple sclerosis for seventeen years. She was sixty-three when she died.

After her death Jane E. Curtis, a Wellesley graduate who said she wished she had known Clara, analyzed some of the poems. Curtis wrote: "The multiple sclerosis that struck her in the prime of life brought the further tragedy of a broken family (her husband did not remain with her); but there was also joy in the faithfulness of her mother, her sister, her sons. [George became a lawyer; Jonathan a violinist with the St. Louis Symphony.] Clara came to terms with the whole tragedy and the torturing question of Job: *Why me?* Part of her reconciliation with fate was the poems, in which she expresses the strong inner life that remained to her during years of total paralysis."

In one poem Clara compares her disease to the bondage of a tyrannical marriage bed. Reading it, I could hear her voice, the mellifluous one. The poem is called "A Marriage." Here is part of it.

> You walked with me on every street
> And jogged my arm and tripped my feet;
> There was a cane, a wheel-chair, then a bed
> And your dominion was complete.
> Now in the bed we lie entwined.
> You are tyrannical but kind,
> Gently you teach my body to obey
> But you do not possess my mind.

Clara Beilor accepted the unacceptable. Her valiant voice still rings in my ears. I hope it always will.

How Did Dr. Eckstein Know Which Canary
Needed the Enema?

I believe that people who shape our lives are given to us. I went to work for Gus Eckstein thanks to my best friend getting pregnant. "But I'll keep working as long as I can," Fifi Keeler told me. The daughter of Cincinnati's famous laryngologist, Dr. Billy Mithoefer, she had the best job in town: Girl Friday for the eccentric celebrity Dr. Gustav Eckstein, professor of physiology at the University of Cincinnati Medical School and author of eight books and three plays.

Ever since our small boys began to lay waste to our house, I had harbored an urge to escape to a demilitarized zone. On a hot July day in the forties, I took a trolley to the medical school for a job interview. I couldn't have imagined the gift I was about to receive.

I may be the only person in the world who has seen a canary get an enema. Dr. Eckstein preferred Shakespeare's word: "clyster." More surprising than the minibird clyster, which he performed deftly with a tiny medicine dropper, was the fact that in a lab full of free-flying canaries, Dr. Eckstein knew which bird needed one. I asked how. Answer: "One learns to see birds as individuals."

On the jacket of *Noguchi*, his biography of the Japanese bacteriologist, Dr. Eckstein compressed his own life into one sentence: "Born, practiced dentistry, studied medicine, taught physiology, learned not much, read two or three men, learned a little, came to know two or three women, learned a good deal, made friends with two rats, learned prodigiously, wrote about rats, continued to write."

I could hardly wait to meet him. The sign on the door of Dr. Eckstein's office read: BIRDS HERE! NO ONE ENTERS UNLESS HIS KNOCK IS ANSWERED. Fifi, great with child, answered my knock and took me in to meet Himself. On the screen door to his office was a yellowing handwritten sign: USE GREAT CARE IN OPENING AND CLOSING THESE DOORS—YESTERDAY, FEBRUARY 23RD, A CANARY SLIPPED OUT, AND ONLY BY THE GRACE OF GOD AND THE WIT AND GENTLENESS OF TWO MEN IS BACK WITH THE FAMILY AGAIN.

In the barren lab, beyond the zinc-topped tables, a little man stood at a draped Steinway grand piano, pounding on a portable typewriter. Twenty or thirty canaries fluttered about him—he did not believe in cages. Occasionally one perched in his wiry gray hair. When he spoke, in a high but undeniably masculine voice, all the birds seemed to vibrate. He was five feet four and weighed a hundred pounds, a vest pocket guru. I loved him on the spot.

"Oh, hello," he said casually. "Fifi will show you how to feed the canaries." He went back to his typing. I wasn't sure he knew why I was there. Fifi told me the canaries got hard-boiled eggs, oranges, apples, lettuce, watercress, and strawberries every day. Sundays they got lemon pie. After my introduction to the birds we had our lunch—broccoli and ice cream. It seemed to me the canaries ate better than he did.

"I never eat meat," Dr. Eckstein said. "As a boy, I peeped through a slaughterhouse window and saw a steer slugged over the head. Turned vegetarian instanter." He talked continuously. "Talk is my intoxication," he announced, looking at the ceiling. Reading *Good Night, Sweet Prince,* a biography of John Barrymore, reminded him of the month he spent on Barrymore's yacht. "A river of filth flowed from Barrymore's mouth, but there was something infinitely sweet about him which Gene Fowler missed. Jesus, what a Hamlet Jack Barrymore was!"

Hamlet, I later discovered, was Dr. Eckstein's Bible. "I never went to college," he said, "but I traveled rapidly through high school and *Hamlet.* Almost blocked by a father who believed in neither. Assisted by a mother who believed in both."

He put down his fork and closed his eyes. "I first read *Hamlet* at age nine in the attic bedroom I shared with Uncle Oscar. You can imagine how well I understood it." He threw back his head and declaimed, "What a piece of work is a man! How noble in reason, how infinite in faculties, in form and moving, how express and admirable, in action how like an angel, in apprehension how like a god—the beauty of the world! The paragon of animals!" He turned to me. "Do you type?"

"Yes," I said, "but not perfectly."

"That's all right. Fi was terrible when she came." Fifi laughed, lamely. After lunch, he held one finger next to his ear, cocked his head, smiled, and vanished into his lab. It was an elfish gesture, not inappropriate in such a lively little man, but what did it mean? Was I hired or not?

Two weeks passed without a word. Should I call? I really wanted that job. Then one day the phone rang and a voice said, "Eckstein here. Fifi has pains. Can you start tomorrow?" I said I could. "Good. What's your first name?" I told him. "Good-bye." He hung up.

Gleefully, I bought a steno notebook and called Mrs. Klosterman, a German hausfrau I had hired to take over the combat zone. My first days on the job were miserable. Every noon I had to feed the crowd of pigeons that fluttered into a huge coop built into a window. "Be sure everyone gets enough," Dr. Eckstein instructed me, "but nobody pigs out." I was supposed to maneuver them in and out by raising and lowering a heavy window on a pulley. Dr. Eckstein knew each bird personally. He would stick his head around the corner and say, "Pinkie's had enough. Shoo her off." Which one was Pinkie? It was a nightmare.

In those p.c. (pre-computer) days, it was all typing. Mine was labored and the script of *The Pet Shop,* Gus's play, complex. (Produced on Broadway, the play lasted only one week.) Between rub-outs, I studied his framed photographs. Dr. Eckstein and Katharine Cornell leaning over a large book. Dr. Eckstein and the Lunts on a log in the woods. Alexander Woollcott as a Chinese mandarin with Harpo Marx as his coolie. Dr. Eckstein with his pet macaw Pawley on his shoulder, caricatured by Covarrubias.

One day Dr. Eckstein got a letter from Helen Keller. She had read his popular book *Canary* in Braille and was going to have *In Peace Japan Breeds War* put into Braille. What sent me home with a sick headache was the faultless, flawless typing — she did her own — of blind Miss Helen Keller.

My job, I soon discovered, continued after hours. One night our phone rang. "My overcoat was stolen while I was eating dinner!" Who would want such a tiny little coat, I wondered. "The keys to my car were in it. You just get one key these days, don't you?"

His lab keys were missing, too. Crucial, because he did all his writing standing at that piano late at night. I sent him my lab keys by taxi and called Fifi (up at midnight nursing Tanny), who located an extra car key. The overcoat turned up later in his closet. "I can't keep track of every goddamned thing," he said.

Part of my job was to wash Dr. Eckstein's underwear, the sleeveless, pongee wraparounds worn by Japanese men. I tried to imagine him in them. I couldn't. Every day Gus — as I learned to call him—wore the same brown corduroy jacket with red bow tie, ragged on just one side. Why? He used to take his small green parrot Vicious to the symphony because "she craved music." He hid her under his coat, and what kept Vicious quiet was chewing on Gus's neckties. Once, during a pause in the music, she erupted in loud squawks and the odd couple was asked to leave.

Gus Eckstein lived intimately with his pet birds, mice, cockroaches. He could tell you which canaries were lazy or angry or sexy, which went to sleep early, which one's feet hurt. He meticulously clocked the habits of all the small creatures who led their skittery lives around his desk. "Canaries are polygamous," he told me, "pigeons monogamous."

From his austere lab in a far-off corner of Ohio, Gus had been drawn into the orbit of the famous and the talented by the critic Alexander Woollcott, grand panjandrum of American literary taste, who read *Canary,* journeyed to Cincinnati to meet the author, and fell for him. Woollcott's cronies embraced Gus as an original. He vacationed with them on Woollcott's fabled island in Lake Bomoseen, Vermont. Moss Hart and George S. Kaufman even wrote him into *The Man Who Came to Dinner,* their zany play that made fun of Woollcott. Gus is Professor Adolph Metz, a wild character with electrified hair—"the world's greatest authority on insect life."

Alexander Woollcott liked to compare Gus Eckstein to Saint Francis, but Gus was no monk. He once planned a rendezvous in Spain with Georgia O'Keeffe, but he fell in love with a witty Irish English teacher named Marty Keegan and canceled out. Georgia O'Keeffe, who had never been to Europe, was furious. She sent him a white feather, emblem of cowardice. Why, oh why, didn't I probe until Gus told me that whole story? Fifty years later, after I published a memorial tribute to Gus, I heard from Georgia O'Keeffe, who was distressed to learn of his death.

Because I dreamed of becoming a writer, I began scribbling down what went on in Gus's magical lab. One morning a tall man knocked and said, "May I come in?" It was Sinclair Lewis, and he stayed all day. Aldous Huxley came too, and Thornton Wilder, but my favorite visitor was Garson Kanin, who only spoke in superlatives. "Gustav Eckstein," he told reporters, "is the best writer in the English language. I've known great men like Franklin Roosevelt and Felix Frankfurter, but beyond question the greatest man I ever met is Dr. Gustav Eckstein." The Cincinnati papers relished that, and so did I. Gus thought it was hilarious.

When Gus's Ford up and died, Kanin and his wife, Ruth Gordon, hired an unemployed actor to dress as a chauffeur and drive a brand new station wagon to Ohio. Gus loved the gift but he was a terrible driver. He was always burning things out. The third time I went to the garage to retrieve his new car, the mechanic said, "That friend of yours is some hot rod driver."

You never knew who might call. Once it was Katharine Cornell, worried about her dachshund's rheumatism. "People take on the personality of their dogs," Gus said afterward. "I myself have always thought of animals as people and people as animals."

The day Helen Hayes walked into the lab, petite and winsome in a new mink coat, the canaries went crazy. She stood wild-eyed as the whirring birds plucked at the fur. Gus ran to reassure her. "That's all right, darling, they're nesting." Reluctantly, he helped her take off the coat. I think he wanted her to let the canaries pick it bald. After she left, he told me he was glad the birds "had the experience of mink."

The secret of Dr. Eckstein's Doctor Dolittle-like intimacy with all living things may have been his profound courtesy. If a canary was hatching eggs in one of the kitchen strainers he provided for nest building, he kept a polite distance, watching with binoculars. Through a microphone wired into the nest, he listened with earphones to a sound new to human ears: the anvil chorus of young bills drilling their way out of an egg. Once he turned to me with tears in his eyes and said, "Who is not moved by a birth?"

He never had any children; his only marriage was doomed by his wife's instability, but relationships had first priority in Gus Eckstein's pared-down existence. He could form a relationship with anybody—a janitor, a corporate lawyer, a bumbling secretary. We all thought we were Gus's best friend. In Conrad's phrase, "He drew people to him by his intensity—it is the gift of the great."

Dr. Eckstein said of his relationship with the white rat who lived in his desk drawer, "I taught Father Rat fondness by being fond." Gus taught me consideration by being considerate. He corrected my work so gently that I thought he was giving me a compliment. When I dropped some books and set off a whirlwind of canaries, Gus knew I was shattered. "Scares occur every hour," he said quietly. "Sometimes all get scared. Sometimes one gets scared and notifies the others. But if a wave of high canary voices sweeps the lab and stillness follows—no head turns, no wing moves—that is canary terror. That, my dear Nardi, we must avoid."

Gradually my relationship with Gus deepened. When word came that my brother, Colonel Red Reeder, had been gravely wounded leading the Twelfth Infantry Regiment ashore at Normandy Beach, Gus suffered almost as much as I did. After Red's leg was amputated, Dr. Eckstein said two sentences I have engraved on my heart. "When life deals you a blow—and it will—if there's nothing you can do, accept it. Once true acceptance takes place, everything changes."

After Red left Walter Reed Hospital, he came to visit us and I took him to meet Gus. I can still see them together—the little doctor with his head thrown back looking up at the athlete with the broad shoulders and the artificial leg. "Change is your enemy, Red," Gus said. "If you can avoid change during this crucial readjustment, you will live longer." He helped Red achieve acceptance. My brother was forced to retire from the army, but instead of brooding he took a writing course. Red Reeder, the one-legged warrior, published thirty-six books and lived to age ninety-four.

Tentatively, timorously, I took Gus some pieces I had written about our family. For a week he didn't say a word. I wished I'd left the damned stuff home. Then one Monday morning, he came in beaming. "Keep writing." To me that was the Nobel Prize for literature.

I loved working for Gus, if you could call it that. But one day Husband was offered a job at *The New York Times*. Should he leave the security of Procter and Gamble for an undiscovered country? He took his dilemma to our Guru. Gus exclaimed, "My God, *The New York Times!* Think of it! Brooks Atkinson! James Reston! You'll thrive on the competition, Tom. Go, by all means, go."

"But Gus, they're writers. I'd be in production."

Silence. Then Gus brightened. "Well," he said, "you can always switch over." Like Emily Dickinson, Gus Eckstein "dwelt in Possibility."

And so the time came to leave Gus's enchanted lab. A lump rose in my throat when I tried to say good-bye. "This is my last day on the job," I said. "I wish I could tell you what working here has meant to me."

"Don't try," he said softly. "You and I don't need words to communicate."

We kept in touch. After the publication of his magnum opus, *The Body Has a Head,* a book he wrote "to make the human body more familiar to anyone who owns one," I watched Gus on the *Today* show. Asked how he had accomplished so much at age eighty-five, he said, "As a boy, I couldn't get over a certain high wall until I stimulated myself with a policeman. Chased by a cop, I cleared that wall with ease. Now death is the cop chasing me. I want to finish my Pavlov book." When Gus visited Pavlov in Leningrad in 1935, the great physiologist authorized him to do a biography. Sad to say, the book was never completed, though *The New Yorker* published a chunk of it.

On his ninetieth birthday, Dick Cavett interviewed him. Gus was still lecturing, advising students, observing birds and animals, staying up until three A.M., playing the piano, studying clouds, rooting for the Cincinnati Reds ("I love the poetry of Pete Rose's quick movements"), writing, researching, conducting seminars, making psychiatric grand rounds at the hospital.

Cavett asked if he were afraid to die. I realize now that Gus's reply was another gift. "If you mean gasping my way out, of course. Agony, I wouldn't like that. But I hope to be present at my own death. Death is just another phase of life. I want to be there to see it. I have a feeling people are too scared to experience it. Hamlet was right: 'The readiness is all.'"

Gus achieved his ambition. He swam in the cold ocean at Nag's Head, North Carolina, and contracted pneumonia. He was flown to the hospital in Cincinnati. Three days later he pronounced himself "on the mend." ("Ills melt," he once wrote me, "when one knows the secret of work.") He got up, dressed, signed himself out, and, escorted by the last of his adoring secretaries, set out for his lab. On the way, he collapsed and died.

Possessions meant nothing to Gus Eckstein, but he bequeathed to those who loved him a unique sense of values. He knew what was important and what was not and lived accordingly, an example of Shakespeare's "action is eloquence." A missionary to the world, he identified with every living thing.

When I heard Gus had died, I picked up *Everyday Miracle* so I could hear his voice. Re-reading his account of the death of the white rat, I could see Gus in his brown jacket and frayed red bow tie, typing at his piano in the lab, a canary perched in his wiry gray hair:

Father grows older and older. Then one evening he leaves drawers and desk top. He goes to be an eagle. I am filled with the pain of the shortness of everything. When I saw his death coming, how truly frightful was the feeling that nothing could stop it. Good care and good food and warmth would save him an uneasy week, perhaps, and were I able to add all the cunning in the world it would save him another week perhaps. How then must I know with a new strong draft of conviction that gentleness and gaiety are the best of life.

The Man Who Started Sociology

When the intellectual history of the twentieth century is com-
piled, the name of David Riesman, the Harvard professor of
social sciences, will be writ large. His seminal work, The
Lonely Crowd: A Study of the Changing American Character,
published in 1950, was a groundbreaker. Written with Nathan
Glazer and Reuel Denney, it explores the changes in middle-
class values and behavior that came with the sudden increase in
leisure, consumerism, mobility, and mass media.

Riesman's words are ingrained in our language. He said
contemporary American values are not "tradition directed" or
"inner directed." Instead, they are more "other directed," looking
to peers and to the media to find out what is right and how to
live. "When tradition-directed people fail," Riesman explained,
"they feel shame in departing from the approved path; the inner-
directed feel guilt for betraying their own principles; the other-
directed feel anxiety over losing the approval of their peers."

Riesman deplored America's trend. "The mass media begin
training children to be consumers before they are two. Today all
little pigs go to market; none stay home; all have roast beef, and
all cry 'we-we-we-we.'"

The great religions all think in terms of connectedness. Everything is related to everything else.   —DAVID RIESMAN, 1909 – 2002

I went to interview Professor Riesman for *Harvard Magazine* when he turned eighty. An unnerving prospect. Who knows enough to converse with David Riesman, one of the brains of the century?

To my delight, I met not an icon but a deeply courteous gentleman who put me at ease. Modest in manner, he was responsive and laughed easily. His wife, Evelyn Thompson Riesman, brought tea and zwieback and vanished. We chatted in the dimly lit, book-inundated parlor-and-music room, with rosy-red curtains and carpet, but who interviewed whom? The world-renowned sociologist, lawyer, scholar, and philosopher was a Questioner. His probing curiosity equaled his dazzling insight.

America was riveted by Riesman's well-documented study of the shift in authority from nineteenth-century dos-and-don'ts to twentieth-century manipulation-and-enticement. *The Lonely Crowd* touched a nerve, with more than a million copies in print in over twenty languages. The book and its sequel, *Faces in the Crowd,* established Riesman as that *rara avis,* an original thinker. For fifty years a steady stream of scholarly publications poured from his pen.

He was a slender man with thinning hair and alert blue eyes behind tortoise-shell glasses. He looked properly professorial in his gray slacks, blue shirt, yellow wool necktie, and baggy tweed jacket with leather elbow patches. Born in Philadelphia on September 22, 1909, he was the first child of intellectual Jewish parents. His mother came from an elegant Philadelphia family; his German-born father was a distinguished professor of medicine at the University of Pennsylvania Medical School.

Riesman saw his parents with a clear eye. "Sarcasm can destroy a young person's confidence. My friends would say, 'You're lucky you have a mother you can talk with.' And I'd say, 'You don't know the half of it.' Imagine a mother who felt she let Bryn Mawr down by having three children. She could get excited over Bach's B Minor Mass and Beethoven's last quartets, and very little else. A formidable aesthete, she didn't think she was first-rate.

"She looked down on people who did the day-to-day work of the world, not excepting my father, who struggled to keep up with her. He was forty-two when I was born, she twenty-seven. It was typical of her that, when she was in analysis with Karen Horney after my father's death, she persuaded me to go into therapy with Erich Fromm, so she would have someone to talk with.

"The old saw says an optimist is one who lives with a pessimist. My doctor-father was an optimist; my scholar-mother inhaled the pessimism of Oswald Spengler's *The Decline of the West.* Her copies of Proust, Joyce, Faulkner, Einstein, and Freud were first editions because she bought them as they came out.

"I can remember my father's delight in opening Christmas presents from grateful patients—I'm still using those handkerchiefs. Mother would sniff, 'Can they be returned?'

"I was a disappointment to parents who learned Italian in order to read Dante. It was not cultivated to know the batting averages of all major league players. Nothing I did was good enough. Creative, intellectual work was for others, not David Riesman, *Junior.*"

Although he did well at Harvard, David wasn't deeply engaged. "I concentrated in biochemistry because my father told me, 'You can get the other things out of books.' At the Liberal Club, I brought to campus a series of innovative college presidents, venturesome men like Alexander Meiklejohn from the University of Wisconsin and Clarence Cook Little from the University of Michigan, who sparked my lifelong interest in education.

"After graduation I went to Russia with an Intourist group led by filmmaker Julien Bryan. At tour's end, Bryan took two of us to a collective farm to discover the disorder beneath the surface of state control and to live uneasily amid the pervasive terror. Since it was harvest time, I went out with a pitchfork to help with the haying—my first such venture. Stepping in a woodchuck hole, I seriously injured my knee and ended up in a Moscow hospital, short on food and medical supplies. For a time my life was in danger."

The former biochemistry major drifted off to Harvard Law School with a hundred others from the Class of 1931. "The Great Depression had no visible impact on my Harvard friends, who sneered at Franklin Roosevelt and claimed anyone who wanted a job could get one." To test this, Riesman went to Detroit in the summer of 1934, his belongings in a poncho slung over his back, dressed in Levi's "before they became the uniform of the affluent young.

"At Ford's River Rouge plant, hundreds applied daily for a dozen jobs. I did not look like a worker, neither then nor later when I applied at the Chicago packing houses. Of course I could not get work." But he did report to his scornful friends that the unemployment crisis was genuine.

He was asked to join the Harvard faculty in 1958: earth-shaking, because he lacked the required doctorate. (When he was eighty-one, Harvard awarded him an honorary degree, finally.) His Social Sciences 136 class was hugely popular. Harvard guru Dr. Robert Coles said, "It took a strong dean like McGeorge Bundy to break the mold and bring David Riesman and Erik Erikson, without Ph.D.'s, to Harvard—a triumph for this university."

When I asked about his wife, David Riesman's eyes shone. "I met Evelyn Thompson—a thoughtful, gentle, beautiful Bostonian—at a Bryn Mawr dance. I fell for her instantly. That summer, my brother, several friends, and I sailed up the coast of Maine. I looked her up in Northeast Harbor and that was it. It's so scary. What if I'd missed her? We couldn't marry for a year because I was to clerk for Justice Brandeis and his clerks did not marry (hard to believe now). In the meantime, Evey became a writer and editor.

"Our marriage has been filled with music. Evey and our four children created a chamber music ensemble. She played the violin and viola; Paul, clarinet; Jennie, violin; Lucy, cello; Michael, oboe and piano. I was the consumer. I am happy to say our grandchildren are musical, too."

An intellectual outlaw, David Riesman was not always popular with the Establishment. Some resented his Cassandra-like prescience. In 1957 he advised Wait Rostow and other Vietnam enthusiasts to adopt a humbler, more modest view of America's role in a diverse world. They didn't listen.

In 1964 Riesman made his first big splash as a seer. He cautioned protesting students at Berkeley: "Aren't you afraid of inducing a backlash? You could produce a right-wing reaction that might make Ronald Reagan governor—or even possibly president!"

I asked him what he foresaw in the future. His reply was, as usual, omniscient. "If our present economic high comes to an end, what kind of meanness and social divisions will follow? The other side of American generosity is vindictiveness. The greatest danger I see ahead," he added, "is the great powers being drawn into a conflict between the nuclear-armed Israelis and their Middle Eastern enemies."

Professor Riesman was a paradoxical thinker. During World War II he broke with close friends who were anti-German, as distinct from anti-Nazi, because he thought them racist. He strongly opposed the Vietnam War but defended the few Harvard students who went to Vietnam voluntarily and were branded war criminals by the radicals. He thought the women's movement the most profound movement of his time, but he opposed the Equal Rights Amendment because he feared tinkering with the Constitution.

David Riesman was called the crown jewel of American education. His wisdom and advice were widely sought; one essay on curriculum reform was titled "What to Do When David Riesman Can't Visit Your Campus." He frequently spoke to workers in the trenches of education, but he refused to appear on TV or radio because he wanted feedback. According to James O. Freedman, the former president of Dartmouth College, Riesman had more to do with the selection of college presidents than anyone else in this country. Riesman himself declined the presidencies of Sarah Lawrence and Reed Colleges because of his "limited capacity for patient leadership."

He fought against homogenization. "Different schools fit different students," he insisted. "Women's colleges and single-sex prep schools are vital, as are black colleges and religious schools." However, he wished all students would be required to learn "two lifelong musical instruments, two lifelong sports, a foreign language, public speaking, and either plumbing or carpentry."

Riesman admits he was born serious. He did not drink or smoke or do crazy things—although as a student he had foolhardy adventures, such as the life-threatening experience of getting lost with a friend on a canoe trip in the Canadian bush.

I learned from David Riesman how to age sensibly. Asked about life at eighty, he said, "I still enjoy some teaching, good movies, and classical music. I've had to give up vigorous tennis and travel—I stay well if I stay put. Above all, I enjoy good conversation. I feel blessed, to have lived so long in reasonably good health, despite diabetes. Evey and I just celebrated our fifty-third anniversary. Our life is felicitous. We see friends at lunch and cocktail parties. We attend most Harvard-related affairs. But we let nothing interfere with our nightly swim at the Belmont Hill Club. We go in the evening and read aloud in the car."

When I asked him about death, David said, "Of course I think about death, not my own so much as the death of family and close friends—the unbearable death at fifty of our oldest son, Paul, very suddenly from an aneurysm is always with me.

"I don't think there is a life after death. It goes against the weight of the evidence. Jewish by birth, I was brought up in an agnostic home. I never entered a synagogue until I attended a classmate's funeral in law school. My parents believed themselves free of religious superstition and practice, but every Sunday my brother, sister, and I were given Bible instruction. Such religion as I had came from years of attending Friends' meetings at the Penn Charter School. I have sympathy with, but not envy for, other people's religions. I take my stand with the Unitarians. I believe in 'one God, if any.'"

David Riesman's overriding preoccupation was with the danger of nuclear war. A lifetime pacifist, he worked tirelessly for peace. "Our planet is in jeopardy. The dangers of the arms race might lead some to personal hedonism and civic inaction, but I'm too much the child of my parents for that. The most important question we face is destructiveness versus love of humanity. Which will prevail?"

Einstein's Mathematician

We first met John Kemeny when Tom came to Dartmouth to create the Parents Fund in 1977. Like everyone else on campus, we were in awe of him. This short man was a giant in intellect. In his fundraising, Tom often took trips with John, who spoke at many Dartmouth occasions. As we got to know him, and saw him relax with his adored wife, Jean, we came to love them both.

The newspaper said John G. Kemeny, thirteenth president of Dartmouth College, died unexpectedly of heart failure. Clearly a mistake. John Kemeny's heart never failed anyone.

At St. Thomas Episcopal Church we prayed for "the eternal rest of President Kemeny's immortal soul." Although he was Jewish, in John Kemeny there was no east or west; no north or south. He was an ecumenical man in the true sense: "of or from the whole world."

All the laudatory obits omitted an important Kemeny facet: his love of teaching. No matter how crowded his schedule, John Kemeny found time to teach. He agreed to become president of Dartmouth on one condition: that he be allowed to continue teaching. The chairman of the trustees said, "The presidency is too demanding." Kemeny asked, "What would you say if I wanted two hours off each week to play golf?" That did it.

It was a poor idea to argue with John Kemeny. Though he was always soft-spoken, even his license plate said LOGIC. He taught two classes a year, ranging from freshman math to far-out computer science. No student ever cut class.

Tom and I once saw John, the brilliant teacher, in action. We attended a 1978 Dartmouth Alumni College course entitled "Where Have All the Heroes Gone?" President Kemeny was invited to speak on his hero. Nobody present will ever forget it. He began by saying that Albert Einstein, a humble scientist who never performed an experiment, had, by just sitting in a room and thinking, changed the entire universe. Then Kemeny went to the blackboard and, using an example of two elevators, taught us the general theory of relativity with breathtaking clarity. He finished with a flourish, writing Einstein's solution on the board: $E=MC2$. We jumped to our feet and thundered an ovation. Effortlessly, John Kemeny had carried three hundred elders beyond their depth and into the elegant world of pure mathematics.

Lu Martin, a special assistant to President Kemeny, told me how he handled his first big crisis. Two months after he took office, the May 1970 bombings in Cambodia and killings at Kent State ignited rage and fear on campuses across the nation. Kemeny rose to the challenge. He canceled Dartmouth classes for the week and led the college in soul-searching and mourning.

The threat of a student strike evaporated. But the Nixon-supporting *Manchester Union Leader* ran a front-page editorial headlined "Dartmouth Has Bought Another Lemon."

"Instantly," Lu Martin said, "lemon tee-shirts blossomed on campus. Students delivered bushels of lemons to the *Union Leader*. They even presented John with a live lemon tree. At the end of the week, John addressed a rally in the fieldhouse. Jean spoke first: 'If you're handed a lemon, John, make lemonade.' She then presented him with a basket of lemons. At the end of his talk, John threw lemons to the wildly cheering crowd."

Like all of us, John Kemeny had shortcomings. He did not suffer fools gladly. He did not moderate his strong opinions or his explosive temper. He did not hide his light under a bushel; he was good and he knew it. To a colleague who suggested that a previous president may have done some things better, Kemeny snapped, "Name one."

Kemeny was not programmed for a college president's hours. A night person, he functioned best after midnight. When he was concentrating on a problem, time never ran out. Once Provost Leonard Rieser ran into him at nine A.M. "John!" he exclaimed, "Why are you on campus at this hour?" "Going home," John replied.

Nor was John one of Dartmouth's outdoorsmen. "My idea of roughing it," he once said, "is a hotel room with only a shower." He once played second base on the Math Department's softball team and was as inept at base running as he was ept at everything else.

John Kemeny grew up in Budapest. To escape the Nazi threat, his family moved to New York in 1940. At thirteen, John Kemeny had never heard a word of English. Three years later he entered Princeton University to study math and philosophy. He took one year off to work on the Manhattan Project in Los Alamos under Richard Feynman. In 1947, Kemeny graduated from Princeton, earning his doctorate two years later.

At age twenty-two, he became Albert Einstein's mathematical assistant. I once asked him why Dr. Einstein needed a mathematician. With that gentle, mustached smile, he said, "Einstein wasn't very good at math."

John Kemeny built the Dartmouth Math Department into a national model. He wrote or co-authored thirteen books on math and philosophy. He established a computer center, the first time-sharing system in the world. With Dartmouth professor Tom Kurtz, he co-authored BASIC, a computer language used internationally.

In 1979 President Carter selected John Kemeny to investigate the Three Mile Island nuclear accident. Kemeny was horrified by the lax conditions he discovered. But as his fellow math maven Laurie Snell put it, "John was a born optimist. He was always sure things could be improved—and they were." A precise scholar, John Kemeny was nevertheless absent-minded. After Ana and Brantz Mayor bought and remodeled the Kemeny's house in Hanover, they invited Jean and John over for cocktails to inspect the changes. "Jean, look!" John exclaimed. "The Mayors added a deck. Great idea!"

"John," Jean laughed, "that deck was here when we were."

Leonard Rieser said John's extraordinary intensity of concentration was the problem. One time they drove to New Haven, where John was to speak. He was giving his topic, the new doctorate of arts in math, his full attention. Rieser finally looked out, "John!" he shouted, "Turn around. We just passed Greenwich!"

"He wheeled around," Rieser recalled, "and we raced toward New Haven. John was proud of his souped-up red car, but it did require gas. He was still expounding when the tank went dry. Then the car overheated. Of course we missed the luncheon. As we walked into the hall, President Kingman Brewster was saying, 'Our next speaker will be John Kemeny.' John walked to the podium and picked up without missing a beat."

John Kemeny's computerized brain retrieved everything except names. That was Jean's department. His dependency on his wife was total. They met when he was twenty-three, she nineteen. She was a freshman at Smith and he, with his new Ph.D., was an assistant professor of philosophy at Princeton. Jean describes their first encounter in her book, *It's Different at Dartmouth*.

"I was going to a United World Federalist Conference at Princeton . . . All the Smithies were to be put up at the houses of professors. We dallied . . . and arrived at two A.M., four hours late. A furious person greeted us—a dreadful person who swore at us! 'God damn it!' was my introduction to John Kemeny."

Jean did not return to Smith for her sophomore year. They married in November 1950.

A member of the Dartmouth search committee told me they struggled over nominating John Kemeny for the presidency. "Because he would be the first non-alum Jewish president?" I asked. "No," the trustee replied. "Because his wife wears slacks."

I have never met a man more pleased with his wife than John Kemeny. In her book Jean writes, "His loyalty is something I can absolutely depend on." The reverse was obviously true. (Their loyal children, Jennie and Rob, went to Smith and Dartmouth.)

After John died, I called Jean. She wanted to talk. "John was a funny and very touching person who communicated better with animals than with people. Our fluffy black cat, Who, followed him like a dog. For fifteen years, John fed our raccoons. Now he's gone, but thirty-five raccoons still come daily to his feeding station on our deck. John used to greet each by name."

Warming to her subject, Jean continued, "He liked science fiction, football games, shrimp, all kinds of puzzles, Agatha Christie, and solitude (for two). He did not enjoy socializing. John recognized only two flowers, the tulip and the rose, and two pieces of music, the 1812 Overture and 'Poor Little Buttercup.' But these last years he has had time to enjoy Mozart, wildflowers, pileated woodpeckers, eclipses. Sometimes he liked to sit still and think. John wasn't a cook, but when I yearned for a Grand Marnier soufflé, he collated all our cookbooks and created a perfect soufflé with *creme anglaise* sauce, just to please me.

"He died the day after Christmas. It all happened so fast. The nausea, the awful pain—and then he just fell. I called 911 and a policeman came. When we got John to the hospital, he had no blood pressure. He was only sixty-six. Jim Strickler [former dean of Dartmouth Medical School] told me later that John's coronary artery was calcified, but in spite of all the smoking, his lungs were clear.

"John and I were two cultures, two countries—a Yankee from Maine and a Jew from Budapest—but," Jean's voice broke slightly, "it worked."

Presiding at his last commencement, John Kemeny presented a diploma to a surly *Dartmouth Review* editor, who handed him a piece of paper. On it the student had written: "Fuck you." President Kemeny did not turn a hair.

At the end, he signaled the dean to raise the senior class. Then, in his soft Hungarian voice, John Kemeny gave his charge to the graduates: "The most dangerous voice you will ever hear is the evil voice of prejudice that divides black from white, man from woman, Jew from gentile. Listen to the voice that says man can live in harmony. Use your very considerable talents to make the world better."

President John G. Kemeny, the ecumenical man, concluded his last commencement exercises with the words he used to end every commencement: "Women and men of Dartmouth, all mankind is your brother—and you *are* your brother's keeper."

The Wisdom of Bill Coffin Is Good for Any Age

I first met Bill Coffin when our oldest son, Tommy, was at Phillips Andover and Bill was the incendiary school chaplain. During his seventeen years as chaplain of Yale, ten years as pastor of New York's Riverside Church, and eight years as president of SANE Nuclear Policy, this dynamic activist has generated enough electricity to ignite many into action, throw others into shock, and blow many fuses.

He marched with Martin Luther King and was one of seven Freedom Riders convicted in 1961 for protesting segregation. Bill's bottom line is that we all must confront the monstrosity of inequality. "The plight of the poor should be at the top of every agenda."

"Contentment," Bill adds, "lies in discerning the value of things we have." He practices what he preaches. Settled into Strafford, Vermont, he is now Guru to the World.

"Bill Coffin," I said, "you are a modern miracle."

He chuckled. "I am alive without my doctor's permission. We all try to forget our days are numbered, but I can't."

When Bill was diagnosed with amylodosis, a threatening heart condition, the doctor told him he had about six months to live. That prophecy had occurred eighteen months earlier.

"There are fringe benefits to being put on notice," he continued. "Recently the Yale Divinity School gave a dinner in my honor—four hundred good friends gathered in one spot. Now I'm looking forward to this weekend, when Gary Trudeau and his wife, Jane Pauley, are coming up to see me." Trudeau, creator of *Doonesbury*, began lampooning George W. Bush when they were both Yale undergraduates. He put Bill into the strip as Reverend Sloan.

My oldest grandson Peter, wife Amy, and new baby Jack had driven me the twenty-odd miles to Strafford to talk with Bill about his new book, *Letters to a Young Doubter.* I wanted him to autograph a copy for my youngest grandson, sixteen-year-old Grady. Almost before I knew it, I had read all 185 pages. It's good for an old doubter, too.

I found Bill sitting in his wicker chair on the front porch of the small cottage he shares with his wife, Randy Wilson, twenty-two years younger than he. They have been married twenty-one years. Like all the Wilsons, Randy is much beloved in Strafford, her hometown. The incomparable Randy brought us iced tea, greeted me warmly, and vanished.

"You're looking trim, Bill," I said. "Losing weight is youth-afying." Impeccably dressed in a new plaid shirt and jeans, he was barefoot. "*Letters to a Young Doubter* is a grandmother's dream. You are so good at communicating with the young about God. I wish you had written it when our kids were growing up."

Like most of our friends, Tom and I brought our children up in a church. Now those baptized and confirmed little Christians, still able to recite the books of the Bible and tell you the difference between St. Luke's sentimentality and St. Mark's austerity, don't feel the need of a church, apparently. Out of five kids I'd guess we have two believers, two skeptics, one unknown. Do they believe in God? How would I know? We never asked them. How dumb can you be?

Bill Coffin, quoting the poet Rilke, tells his correspondent, a college freshman, "Love the questions and live into the answers . . . You have a lifetime, but start now."

I think—I hope—all of our children seek the life of the spirit and nurture it. But I regret that when they were growing up we rarely discussed it. Coffin quotes St. Benedict: "God often shows what is better to the younger." Had my husband and I talked with them about the *mysterium tremendum,* we might have learned something.

The Reverend Coffin once told a gathering of Yale faculty skeptics, "I understand doubting the quality of the bread, but I can't see kidding yourself that you're not hungry—unless your soul has so shriveled up, you have no appetite left for the great mysteries of life."

Bill, who was a paratrooper in World War II and a leader of draft-card burning during the Vietnam War, bitterly opposed the Iraq War. "Human beings never do evil so cheerfully as when they do it for religious conviction," he wrote, quoting Pascal. Coffin cited the self-righteousness of Christian Crusaders against the Muslims, and present-day "American Christians who cheered President Bush's messianic militarism."

"Which is worse," he asked, "the intolerance that commits outrages, or the indifference that observes outrages with an undisturbed conscience?"

The Reverend Coffin left Yale to become pastor of New York's famous nondenominational Riverside church. A deeply committed Christian, he remains on the wavelength of doubters, old and young. "In my experience," he wrote, "a religious faith despite doubts is far stronger than one without doubts."

One of the potent questions Bill asked the young doubter was, "Who tells you who you are?" As a mother, only once can I remember telling an offspring who he was, and that didn't work too well. Russell, age six, let out a string of cuss words. "Russell!" I cried, "You are a Campion, and Campions don't swear." (What did I know?) Russell: "I'd rather be a Ransom and swear." The Ransoms were the next-door neighbors, who had six boys and three subscriptions to *Playboy*.

Bill Coffin arrived at one of his deepest insights the hardest way. In 1983, his son Alex and a friend were celebrating an intense tennis match at a pub in South Boston. They left during a terrible rainstorm. Alex's wipers weren't working well and the road was unlit. As Bill put it, "The road took a ninety-degree turn and Alex kept going straight. He drove into Boston Harbor. The buddy escaped. My guess is that Alex hit the windshield as the car went down. He probably was out cold and never came to."

Speaking about the "grief work" that helped him survive, Bill wrote, "You don't reach my age without shedding a Niagara of tears. Tears are God-sent to cleanse the heart of bitterness."

Bill Coffin is an original thinker and a great quoter. There are a lot of quotes in this book—but what quotes! Reverend Coffin only consorted with the best. Take *Moby Dick*. Talking about how all wise people think tragically, because tragedy teaches us to reflect, Bill recalled Melville's words: "Rainbows do not visit clean air; they only irradiate vapor." He added, "The heart would see no rainbow had the eye no tears."

At the end of *Letters to a Young Doubter*, Bill Coffin told his freshman correspondent, "You are on your way to fulfilling the calling of every human being, which is to live a life worth the retelling of it."

A fair description of Bill Coffin's own life.

In the Senate Dining Room
with Senator Clinton

"Women are on the move!" my mother cried in 1920. At long, long last the Nineteenth Amendment had passed and women, those third-class citizens, were finally allowed to vote. I was three years old and had been shouting with a clenched fist, "Votes for Women!" since I could talk.

I hate to think of this country bobbling along for two centuries without women legislators. Wellesley College is leading the movers with one secretary of state and one U.S. senator. Yet even today there are only a handful of women in Congress. Eventually many more women will be heard.

My favorite senator is making history, and will continue to do so.

Russell answered the phone. The family was gathered in my apartment before Tom's memorial service in December 2000. "This is Russell Reeder Campion."

"This is Hillary Rodham Clinton."

"Oh, hi, Hillary," Russell said, as if the first lady (as she then was) called everyday. I jumped up and ran to the phone. Hillary had read Tom's obit in *The New York Times*. She offered condolences, then said: "I admire the way you and Tom lived your life together."

That meant a lot to me and I told her so, adding, "I am so proud of Wellesley's First Senator."

"Come see me in the Senate," she laughed, "and I'll take you to lunch."

A few months later, three of us dined in style in the Senate Dining Room on what turned out to be a historic day. Hillary had invited our dear friend, Priscilla Dewey Houghton, to join us. She is the wife of Amo Houghton, for eighteen years the Republican congressman from New York's 31st Congressional District. He grew up in Corning, New York.

Priscilla and I waited excitedly in a small reception room off the dining room. We jumped up when Hillary walked in, trim in her black suit, flesh-colored shell, pink faux pearls, and earrings. TV doesn't do justice to her peaches-and-cream complexion, large blue eyes, highlighted blonde hair, and smile that is warm and cool at the same time.

Though fully aware of her star power, I was surprised when we walked into the Senate dining room. Voices hushed, heads swiveled. You'd think they'd be used to her by now. There may be Hillary haters out there, but when she shows up they melt away. Being in her presence at the Senate strengthened my first impression: she is unflappable. And I mean Presence; that's what she has.

The dining room was plush: centered by a huge crystal chandelier, with floor-to-ceiling windows, tieback green velvet draperies, red oriental carpeting, and gold-framed portraits on pinkish-beige walls. That day, the room was bristling with bigwigs: John McCain, Christopher Dodd, Arlen Specter, Barbara Boxer, Phil Gramm, Richard Lugar. Some of the men with new-for-TV facelifts looked as if they had on rubber face masks.

Everyone was present, and the air was crackling with subdued excitement. It was "Jim Jeffords Day," May 23, 2001. The seismic boom of Republican Senator Jeffords's switch was still reverberating. By becoming an Independent, this one man had shifted control of the Senate from the Republicans to the Democrats.

We were in the eye of the storm. The Senate teemed with reporters and television cameras, but no Senator Jeffords. Broadcasters, always hyping it up, were claiming Jeffords's decision still hung in the balance. Hillary laughed, "Oh, Jim's just gone up to Vermont. He wants to make the announcement to his own people, which is right." No gloating, that's not her style. "We'd better order. I have to be on the floor in an hour to vote on the Republican's terrible tax bill that will help the rich and cause so much damage to the economy."

I asked why nobody paid attention to all the programs for the needy the huge tax cut would decimate. The senator shook her head. "We've talked about that until we're blue in the face, but for some reason the media just isn't interested. A program for the poor becomes a poor program."

The staff in the dining room hovered around Hillary. She had crab cakes; Priscilla, Caesar salad; I had the best soft-shell crabs I've ever tasted. We sipped iced tea and talked about everything.

Chelsea, who was about to graduate from Stanford ("Tobias Wolf was one of her favorite teachers") was traveling in Ireland with her dad. "She passed all the pre-med courses, then fell in love with history. This fall she's going to Oxford to get a master's degree. We are so blessed."

We fell silent. Hillary asked, "How's my Hanover friend Dr. Koop?"

"Going full-blast at eighty-five."

She switched to books. "I can't wait to read David McCullough's book on John Adams. Adams and Madison were overshadowed; they never got their due. I'm not so crazy about Thomas Jefferson. He was a genius, but slippery."

Hillary was forthright about missing the White House. "That seems like another life, a totally other, wonderful life. There's no place like the White House. But once you're out of the White House, you're out. That's the way it is." She said she loves Washington, the beauty of it, the greenness of it.

"This is another life, too. I love my job. I'm happy here. But I miss the joys of White House travel. At the Beijing World Conference in 1995 Chelsea and I met women from 185 countries."

I spoke up. "One sentence from your speech at that conference ought to go into *Bartlett's Quotations:* 'Human rights are women's rights and women's rights are human rights.'"

"Thanks for remembering. Chelsea and I went everywhere, working for women. The abuses against them are as despicable as they are widespread. It's upsetting, but we had fun, too. We rode elephants in India, hunted big game with cameras in Africa." She turned to Priscilla. "Amo does good work getting his side of the aisle in line on Africa. Most Republicans are not interested in Africa."

Priscilla beamed. "Amo says you ran a great campaign, Hillary. You visited every small town in upstate New York."

"I love the rural part of New York. It's beautiful up there."

We talked about women who are Democrats married to Republicans, and Hillary said something I'm still mulling over: "I think most women are Democrats in their hearts."

During lunch the Senator got up twice to speak to people at other tables; you could almost see the chosen puff up. People visited our table, too. Hillary remembers everybody's name, of course. A gray-haired woman presented her with a book she'd just written about her famous father. Hillary introduced us. "This is Sharon Robinson, Jackie's daughter. Sharon directs educational programs for the baseball commissioner."

Hillary has changed since I first met her ten years earlier. She is wiser. She's better looking. She never used to give a hoot what she wore; now she's turned out. She's more self-confident and has more small talk. But she's not as open as she was when I first got to know her during the 1990 presidential campaign.

Not surprisingly, over the years she has developed a polite way of keeping people at arm's length.

As always, we laughed a lot. She poked fun at those brazen men who think they are the ones who should legislate a woman's choice. Hillary keeps her humor under wraps; women politicians are expected to be serious.

This may be changing. In a speech at Yale's Class Day, Senator Clinton laughed at the media's fascination with her hairdos: "The most important thing I have to say to you is that hair matters. This is a life lesson my family did not teach me, Wellesley and Yale Law School failed to instill: your hair will send significant messages to those around you. Pay attention to your hair, because everyone else will."

We had to hurry our dessert. Over charlotte russe (delish) I said, "Hillary, if I ask you two questions, will you give me the unvarnished truth?"

"I'll try."

"One: are you the most famous woman in the world? Two: if you aren't, who is?"

She threw back her head and laughed. "Madonna."

"That won't do," I said. "Think of India and Africa."

"How about Queen Elizabeth?"

"Not in South America. You just have to accept it as a fact, Hillary. You are the most famous woman in the world."

She shrugged. "I hadn't really thought of that."

My self-confidence was picking up. "I'm psychic," I declared. "One day you will return to the White House. I know it; in your bones you must know it. Someday a woman is going to be elected president of the United States and where could they find a woman as qualified as you are? I just hope I live to see it."

"If it ever happens," she laughed, "I'll give you the first interview." I can't wait for that phone call.

In February 2003, Wellesley (finally!) presented Hillary with its Alumnae Achievement Award. I was asked to give the toast to her at the banquet. Nervous-making, but exciting. I began by saluting Hillary as a mother—what a challenge it is to raise a child in the White House. Chelsea, a poised young woman with an ego in balance, had just been awarded a master's degree in international relations at Oxford. Chelsea is a tribute to her parents.

My Toast to H.R.C.

I want to propose a toast to Wellesley's First United States Senator— the first senator from *any* woman's college—a woman who adds new luster to the word woman. Her strongest characteristic, I believe, is calmness at the center. That inner calm stems from a deep spiritual life, nurtured by Bible study at Wellesley, enriched by her pursuit of solitude and tranquillity. She passes Kipling's test with all flags flying. I hope Rudyard isn't whirling in the grave over my feminization of his poem.

> If you can keep your head when all about you
> Are losing theirs and blaming it on you . . .
> If you can meet with triumph and disaster
> And treat those two impostors just the same . . .
> Or, being lied about, don't deal in lies,
> Or, being hated, don't give way to hating,
> Or, walk with kings—nor lost the common touch . . .
> Yours is the Earth and everything that's in it,
> And—which is more—you'll be a woman my girl.

I give you Wellesley's own United States Senator, Hillary Rodham Clinton.

Who knows what she'll do next?

Cyber Grandma Goes to Town

My kids' mantra used to be, "Ask Granny, she'll do it." And she would, too. My mother would play "choo choo" with little Tommy; spend endless hours looking at Tad's stamp collection; cheerfully endure Toby's Beatles records; and help Cissa memorize rule after rule of "A Girl Scout is . . ."

But it was her youngest grandchild, Russell, who received her total indulgence. Every spring vacation Granny sent Russell a roundtrip ticket to Virginia. She got him a private room at Old Point's Chamberlin Hotel, where she lived, and gave him room service privileges. "That was when I learned," Russell recalls, "that hamburgers and french fries taste better at three A.M."

I fall far short of my role model but I keep trying. From Ashley's umpteen photographs of baby Anna to Maddy's funny and original e-mails and every amazing grandchild in between— Berit, Peter, Manolo, Ned, Iris, and Grady—I can't get enough of them. Now I've fallen in love with their loves—Matt Semler, Amy Thomas, and Michelle Grey. Grandchildren are the gift that keeps on giving.

Tom used to call grandchildren "the real payoff," but he didn't know the half of it, alas. Oh those great-grandchildren! I am overboard about Matt and Ashley's Anna, her arms swinging, charging into rolling surf dressed only in her floppy white hat; and our Buddha, Peter and Amy's unruffleable baby Jack. Not to mention the eager anticipation of great-grandchild number three, the Semlers' second child (sex unknown by parental choice). Soon I will have three Greats. Bliss beyond compare. How could I be so lucky?

Cyber Grandma Goes to Town

At Wellesley College I took to heart the sentence in gold above the altar: "God is love." By the logic of my heart, I can easily extrapolate to my grandchildren, whom I also worship and say, "Grandchildren are love."

"How did you go to New York?"

"By Internet, what else—my granddaughter Ashley is the Duchess of Internet."

My big adventure began with an e-mail from grandchild number one, who lives in California. Having started with inkwells and dip pens, I especially enjoy e-mail. It's the only way to communicate with your grandkids. They don't do post office, just "buddy list." Luckily, grandchild number two, Berit, taught me all I needed to know to be a cyber grandma. Ashley and Berit are both Dartmouth-trained computer freaks.

Ashley's e-mail: "Guess what, Gama, I'm flying east for your birthday." In those pre–September 11 days, kids used to hop planes the way Tom and I hopped trolleys. "Can you meet me in New York? Flight's on me. We're going to celebrate your birthday at *The Producers.* I think. I'm still working on the tickets."

"Hooray!" I e-mailed. "Tell me more about *The Producers.*"

She faxed a review from NYTimes.com. I, who started with three-cent stamps, am on the fax track, too. "Mel Brooks's megahit musical *The Producers* is fast, fierce, shameless, vulgar, and altogether blissful. It opened April 19, 2001. The next day three million dollars worth of tickets were sold. Want tickets? Try 2002."

I e-mailed: "Are you talking my birthday in 2002? Do you want to take your grandmother to a 'fierce, shameless, vulgar' show?"

Ashley: "I'm talking next week. Listen, Gama, you're shock-proof." Flattery will get you everywhere. I signed on for the birthday blast, tickets or no. Ashley is the Can-Do Kid.

Variety.com told me, "Tickets for *The Producers*—if you can get them—are $100 apiece at the box office, a Broadway record." Ye gods, in 1950 when Tom took me to *The Lady's Not for Burning,* with John Gielgud and Richard Burton, tickets were $2.50 each (and a 20 cent tax). Box office price fifty years from now? Don't even ask.

Ashley e-mailed unnerving instructions. "You have an E-ticket waiting at Lebanon Airport." Travel by virtual ticket? Tickets from Virginia to Massachusetts on the C&O railroad were three feet long. Ashley left California sans theater tickets and I left home sans plane tickets.

Guess what: the E-ticket worked. Hello, Cyber Grandma. Thank you, Can-Do Kid.

Ashley called across the hotel lobby. "Got the theater tix! My Palm Pilot (related to Palmolive soap?) says we pick 'em up at the box office an hour before the show. They'll be there. I think." Again I held my breath. Again tix were there. Cyber G. is developing new faith in the invisible.

How did the Can-Do Kid do it? Money doesn't dent this smasheroo. You have to know somebody who knows somebody. Ashley wouldn't divulge details. "No cash changed hands. I just kept e-mailing a wheeler-dealer who owes me one. She came through—finally—because it's my grandma's eighty-fourth birthday." Ashley gave me a big hug. (Oh, to be eighty-four again.)

We walked to the theater because Internet Ashley had down-loaded directions on Mapquest.com. Cyber Grandma's feet began to hurt.

The theater lobby was clubby. New Yorkers love shows you can't get into. A man in a Yale tie quipped, "Getting into *The*

Producers is like being tapped for Skull and Bones, only better." A complete stranger asked me, "How did you get *your* tickets?" I replied, "Just lucky. I have grandchildren."

The Producers has one huge advantage: the audience comes ready to laugh, no matter what. They start giggling as the curtain rises and never stop. For good reason. Nathan Lane was over the top. He played Max Bialystock (Yiddish for "hick"), the manic producer who created Broadway hits like "The Kidney Stone" and "Breaking Wind." But, alas, Max, who once made *Hamlet* into a musical, is now a has-been.

Matthew Broderick was Max's sidekick, Leo Bloom, striving to be sophisticated. But in moments of stress Leo opens his briefcase and whips out his blankie.

Max and Leo decide they can make more money with a flop than a hit. (Take all the cash you raised and run.) Hunting for the world's worst play, they discover a surefire flop called *Springtime for Hitler.* We are treated to this turkey, where Geriatric Rockettes kick, not legs, but aluminum walkers. Hotsytotsy Nazis march, stamp, *Sieg Heil,* crooning sentimentally, "Springtime for Hitler and Germany, winter for Poland and France."

Then disaster sets in. Against all odds, their "flop" is so terrible that it's a hit. Mournfully, Max and Leo sing, "Where Did We Go Right?" But you can't keep a bad man down long. As the police trundle Bialystock and Bloom off to prison, they belt out, "I gotta Sing-Sing / I gotta Sing-Sing."

You can see Mel Brooks's 1968 film *The Producers* on video, sans music, or hear the Broadway music on CD. But it's the combo of the goofy story, the two way-out stars, plus the catchy tunes with risqué lyrics that is deliciously overwhelming. It's like standing under Niagara Falls. Add to the mix one giggling granddaughter, and the experience itself goes over the top.

Is *The Producers* worth all the hoorah? Wild roller coaster rides aren't for everybody. The woman next to us complained, "Adolph Hitler is not funny." I was tempted to repeat Mark Twain's line, "Against the assault of laughter, nothing can stand."

After the show I half expected a taxi summoned by double-click. No taxis. The Can-Do Kid and Cyber Grandma trudged up Eighth Avenue. Now C.G.'s feet really hurt. A limo stopped and the driver called, "Want a ride, ladies?" I exhaled a sigh of relief.

C.D.K.: "How much to 59th and 5th?"

Driver: "Ten dollars."

C.D.K.: "I'll give you five."

"No way." I tried to smile bravely. We plodded on. Driver honked. "How about seven?" We zoomed to our hotel in style, but too late for my feet.

Flying back to Lebanon, I felt "with it." I had gone to town by Internet. I learned that Web and bug aren't insects, Yahoo isn't a hillbilly, and uplink is a word. But the best part of my mega-birthday at the mega-hit-of-the-millennium was the mega-hug from my granddaughter. Now all I have to worry about is Ashley and Berit whisking me to Mars for my hundredth birthday.

At Home.com—Harvest Hill Retirement Community— Cyber Grandma went into recovery. If laughter is the best medicine, why was she done in?

I turned off my computer, my fax, my copier, my telephone, my answering machine. I propped up my throbbing feet, sipped my hot tea, and drifted into the lovely lo-tech past. There was Tom beaming at two grinning grandsons, each holding up a wet trout. He was saying, "Grandchildren are the real payoff."

Epilogue

With Attention in Your Heart

As I creak toward birthday eighty-nine, my horizon is fogged by uncertainty, but I know for sure I am headed into challenging territory. An acute awareness of my own mortality puts an edge on my sense of values. This can be unnerving, but it is also invaluable.

I cling to a letter I received from my professor of Old and New Testament at Wellesley. After her lifetime companion, Professor Mary Jean Lanier, died, Seal Thompson wrote, "Depression haunts me. Only two things help, prayer and counting your blessings." Prayer and counting your blessings, yes.

Professor Thompson was a Quaker. For her, prayer did not mean thinking up and asking. Prayer meant thinking in and listening. As my friend and neighbor, New York's Riverside Church Pastor Dr. Harry Emerson Fosdick, once told me, "When I pray I get down on my knees and say, 'Now God . . . ' Then I wait."

Buddhists call this "listening with the heart." Drawing closer to the fearsome unknowable, I strive for sacred listening. Sad to say, kneeling is no longer an option. Happy to say, I am still able to walk. So what if I wobble? I have a sturdy cane. Secretly I think of it as sacred walking. I attempt sacred resting, too. Not too successful, as I cork off rapidly.

Sacred is a word that turns some people off. My dear friend Jim Brodhead, who insists he is an atheist, rejects the word entirely. Yet when I ask him, "Do you believe in the life of the spirit?" he replies, "Music means everything to me." I let that go. I know better than to discuss faith with Jimmy. But music, along with acts of kindness, heavy snowfalls, and blazing sunsets, can open our hearts to Possibility. Heard melodies are sweet, but those unheard are sweeter.

There are some things in life one simply has to accept. They may feel unacceptable—aging and death, for instance—but acceptance can make all the difference. Once complete acceptance takes over, everything changes.

Theophan the Recluse, a nineteenth-century saint in the Russian Orthodox Church, wrote in *Seeking God,* "One act is required—and that is all: for this one act pulls everything together and keeps everything in order . . . This one act is *to stand with attention in your heart.*"

My military childhood led me to read that as "*at* attention," ready to take orders. In my old age, I know that "*with* attention in your heart" means to be open to whatever lies ahead. The ultimate acceptance goal, not easy but so worth striving for, is to achieve Joseph Campbell's "joyful participation in the sorrow of life."

It has finally dawned on me that growing up and growing old are the same thing. It is what we are meant to be doing all our lives.